About Island Press

Since 1984, the nonprofit Island Press has been stimulating, shaping, and communicating the ideas that are essential for solving environmental problems worldwide. With more than 800 titles in print and some 40 new releases each year, we are the nation's leading publisher on environmental issues. We identify innovative thinkers and emerging trends in the environmental field. We work with world-renowned experts and authors to develop cross-disciplinary solutions to environmental challenges.

Island Press designs and implements coordinated book publication campaigns in order to communicate our critical messages in print, in person, and online using the latest technologies, programs, and the media. Our goal: to reach targeted audiences—scientists, policymakers, environmental advocates, the media, and concerned citizens—who can and will take action to protect the plants and animals that enrich our world, the ecosystems we need to survive, the water we drink, and the air we breathe.

Island Press gratefully acknowledges the support of its work by the Agua Fund, Inc., Annenberg Foundation, The Christensen Fund, The Nathan Cummings Foundation, The Geraldine R. Dodge Foundation, Doris Duke Charitable Foundation, The Educational Foundation of America, Betsy and Jesse Fink Foundation, The William and Flora Hewlett Foundation, The Kendeda Fund, The Andrew W. Mellon Foundation, The Curtis and Edith Munson Foundation, Oak Foundation, The Overbrook Foundation, the David and Lucile Packard Foundation, The Summit Fund of Washington, Trust for Architectural Easements, Wallace Global Fund, The Winslow Foundation, and other generous donors.

The opinions expressed in this book are those of the author(s) and do not necessarily reflect the views of our donors.

Biophilic Cities

Timothy Beatley

Biophilic Cities

*Integrating Nature into
Urban Design and Planning*

Timothy Beatley

Washington | Covelo | London

Library of Congress Cataloging-in-Publication Data

Beatley, Timothy, 1957–
     Biophilic cities: integrating nature into urban design and planning / Timothy Beatley.
          p.   cm.
     Includes bibliographical references and index.
     ISBN-13: 978-1-59726-714-4 (cloth : alk. paper)
     ISBN-10: 1-59726-714-7 (cloth : alk. paper)
     ISBN-13: 978-1-59726-715-1 (pbk. : alk. paper)
     ISBN-10: 1-59726-715-5 (pbk. : alk. paper)
   1. City planning—Environmental aspects.   2. Sustainable development.
3. Human ecology.   4. Urban ecology (Sociology)   I. Title.
     HT166.B3927 2010
     307.1'216—dc22

                         2010011658

Printed using Bembo and Korinna

Printed on recycled, acid-free paper

Manufactured in the United States of America
10 9 8 7 6 5 4 3 2 1

Keywords: biological diversity, biomimicry, biophilia hypothesis, bioregional planning, ecocity, environmental education, green building, green urbanism, green streets, light pollution, nature deficit disorder, stormwater management, sustainable, community design, urban ecology, urban parks, urban planning and design

To Jadie and Carolena,

and the next generation of urbanites

who will care about the nature around them.

Contents

Preface

This book is a first effort at explicating and tentatively defining what a *biophilic* city is and what it might look and feel like. While the title will be a bit unfamiliar to planners and urban designers today, part of the purpose for writing this book is to change that and to squarely place connections with and care for nature in urban areas on the agenda for these disciplines.

There are several parallel geneses of this book that should be credited. The first is a highly stimulating conference organized by Professor Stephen Kellert, through the auspices of the Yale School of the Environment, in the spring of 2006. It brought together an amazing "who's who" of theoreticians and practitioners in the area of green design. The presentations were innovative and heady, and it felt very much like we were collectively breaking new ground, and we were. The outcome of that meeting was the subsequent publication of the groundbreaking book *Biophilic Design: The Theory, Science and Practice of Bringing Buildings to Life*,[1] edited by Kellert, along with Judith Heerwegen and Marty Mador.

Biophilic Design has been very well received, especially within the architectural community, and there is no other book quite like it. But it is heavily focused on buildings. I was asked to write a chapter in that book on biophilic cities, and it is one of the only pieces that extend the discussion beyond the structure, building, and site. The Kellert book was a tremendous advancement to the design literature but served to further convince me of the need for a stand-alone book about biophilic cities, which you now hold in your hands.

This book is also intended to serve as a companion (of sorts) to the 2009 documentary film *The Nature of Cities* (*NOC*). The making of this film has served as another important point of learning and inspiration for the book. Special thanks are due my Colorado-based filmmaker–collaborator Chuck Davis, whose creative eye and stimulating questions helped to propel this book forward as well. Chuck's last film, *Transforming Energy*, received critical acclaim and was widely aired on PBS stations around the country, and there is every expectation that *NOC* will be equally successful as it airs in the months and years ahead. But while the book benefits from the film and tracks it in many ways, it is broader and more inclusive, tackling issues (such as what precisely a biophilic city is), stories, and examples not covered in the film (or that could not be adequately covered in a short documentary film). Nevertheless the two are quite complementary and should be seen as useful companions. The film is a visual and sensory celebration of the green and natural qualities of many cities and features faces and smiles and wondrous looks on people living and working on the greening of their cities, and this is a useful thing indeed.

What follows is a relatively compact book, modeled after E. O. Wilson's *The Creation*[2]—beautifully written and illustrated, provocative and thoughtful, and highly accessible. I'm not sure if I've reached these lofty aspirations, but I have given a try. The subject deserves nothing less.

As will be apparent, the book draws heavily on the actual conditions, experiences, and programs under way in a number of cities around the world. The bulk of the examples and stories, however, are from North American, European, and Australian cities where the author's own work has focused. This is a limitation and one I hope will be addressed (perhaps by others) as the ideas and concepts of biophilic cities and biophilic urbanism catch on and move forward. Are these ideas and design and planning expressions as easily applied in larger cities of the developing South, for instance? How relevant is biophilic design to the billion or so residents of slums in large cities around the world. Will biophilia have any practical meaning or use in the favelas (slums or shantytowns) of São Paulo or Rio de Janeiro or the shantytowns in cities like Lagos in Nigeria or Mumbai (formerly Bombay). Indeed, the issues of balancing nature and human needs are undoubtedly different in those locations. As I am writing, a conflict has arisen in Rio over the building of a series of walls separating favelas from surrounding remnants of the very biodiverse Atlantic forest, ostensibly to prevent further encroachment. In Mumbai, for instance, population growth and urban expansion have virtually eliminated the diverse system of mangroves that protected that urban estuary from floods. In other megacities, such as Mexico City, smog and air pollution take priority on the environmental agenda. Despite the severity of these urban problems, it is my hope that the goals and aspirations of biophilic cities, the desire to create the conditions of urban life in close contact with the natural world, will prove relevant and compelling throughout the world, but that will have to await future writing and research and the works of others to follow.

In that vein it is worth emphasizing that what follows here is not the definitive work on what the biophilic city is or could be. Rather, the goal is much more modest: to at least begin to talk about what a biophilic city might include or feel like or look like. It's meant to be more exploratory than thorough, more provocative than comprehensive. I will await others who will pick up the gauntlet and carry through with what will likely be more ambitious agendas and scholarship. I am happy to mark an important beginning in thinking about cities through a biophilic lens.

What follows are six chapters that together begin to sketch out what a biophilic city is or could be. Chapter 1 explores the history and meaning of the concept of biophilia and how it might be useful in shaping the design and planning of cities. A number of arguments are made on behalf of efforts to integrate nature into cities and urban neighborhoods. Chapter 2 is an exploration of the wondrous and amazing nature that does in fact exist in cities; from the microscopic to the large, from the visual to the auditory, from the discrete to the enveloping, nature is everywhere and ubiquitous, though often hidden and unnoticed by urbanites. Chapter 3 is an initial attempt at defining what a biophilic city is, or might be, and what some of its main qualities and key principles are. What does a biophilic city look and feel like, and what are its sensibilities and values?

A number of specific strategies for planning for and designing in nature are examined in chapter 4, with many examples offered from North American, European, and Australian cities. From larger-scale plans for restoring natural systems and green infrastructure to the site level and building scale, this chapter provides a comprehensive introduction to the state of the practice in biophilic urban design. Chapter 4 also explores the design and functioning of biophilic urban neighborhoods. Again with many examples of existing neighborhoods across the country and world, the main question is, What will be necessary to make nature a (the) central organizing element of the urban places in which we live and play and raise children? Chapter 5 is an exploration of what is needed beyond physical design and planning— what are the institutions and organizations, the urban capabilities, the grant programs and new urban codes needed to stimulate and in some cases mandate biophilic cities and urban design. Finally, chapter 6 provides concluding remarks and some speculations about future directions in research and practice in the area of biophilic cities.

Foreword

Beautiful, benevolent, and soul restoring, nature waits for us to bring her home.

It is not so much that humanity has destroyed a large part of the natural world and withdrawn from the remainder. We have also expelled it needlessly from our daily lives. Today, the number of people living in urban areas has passed the number living in rural areas. Simultaneously, the home range of each person on average, the area traversed on a regular basis, is declining steadily. In the cities we do not grow our own food or hunt for it. Mostly, we pick it up at a market and have little idea of its origin. Our eyes are fastened upon the digitized images of screens. Even the images of nature we see are those of remote places, taken by other people.

No matter, we say—the city sustains us, and we are happy. But so are cattle in a feedlot. They are provided with the essentials of maintenance but can never live the lives true to their species and the epic million-year evolution that put them on Earth. They cannot visit the habitat in which they were born. They cannot roam freely, explore, learn the dangers and discover the delights that shaped their bodies and brains. And to a lesser degree, the same is true of humans in most of the cities around the world.

Cities—rural villages in the beginning—have been in existence for only about ten thousand years, and then for most of the ensuing time for only a very small percentage of the population. In *Biophilic Cities: Integrating Nature into Urban Design and Planning,* Timothy Beatley shows that in creating them, we have carelessly left out part of the environment vital to the full development of the human mind. The evidence is compelling that frequent exposure to the natural world improves mental health, it offers a deep sense of inner peace, and, in many ways we have only begun to understand by scientific reason, it improves the quality of life.

Beatley also demonstrates the many ways to design urban landscapes and buildings to bring nature into the hearts of our cities. He shows the effect of even little changes in health and economic growth. The cost is relatively little to further such a readaptation to the rest of the living world, and the potential benefits are enormous.

Edward O. Wilson

One

The Importance of Nature
and Wildness in Our Urban Lives

For several years now I have been administering an interesting slide-based survey to my new graduate students. I call it the "what is this?" survey, and it consists largely of images of flora and fauna native to the eastern United States. Interspersed are other images, political and corporate. I ask students to tell me everything they can about the images I present, and the results are usually rather discouraging: Few students are able to name even common species of birds, plants, or trees. Sometimes the results are amusing (and would be more so if they weren't so sad).

One image I present is of a silver-spotted skipper, a very common species of butterfly. Many students identified it as a moth (not unreasonable), some a monarch butterfly (it looks nothing like a monarch, but apparently this is the only species of butterfly some Americans know of), and several students even thought it was a hummingbird. Only one student in several hundred has correctly identified the species. For me the results confirm what I already knew: For most of the current crop of young adults, nature is fairly abstract and rather general. They grew up in an age of computer games, indoor living, and diminished free time. It is probably not surprising that common species of native flora and fauna are not immediately recognizable, but it is an alarming indicator of how we have become disconnected from nature.

Fortunately the students do not have a blasé attitude about this but, encouragingly, a sense of genuine concern about how poorly they fared on this unusual test.

I'm certainly not the only one to notice the limited knowledge of our youth about the natural world and to wonder what this might bode for the future of community and environment. Paul Gruchow, a notable Midwest writer and essayist, has been one of the most eloquent observers of this trend. He tells the story of the local town weed inspector who arrives at his home, in response to a neighbor's complaint about an unkempt yard, only to be unable to identify any of the offending plants and shrubs in the yard (all of which Gruchow knew, and knew well). More disturbing, Gruchow found that a group of high school seniors he took on a nature walk to a nearby lake were unable to name or recognize even the most common midwestern plants. Gruchow connects this to love, that essential thing that binds and connects us to one another and to the places and natural environments that make up our home. "Can you," Gruchow asked those students, "imagine a satisfactory love relationship with someone whose name you do not know? I can't. It is perhaps the quintessential human characteristic that we cannot know or love what we have not named. Names are passwords to our hearts, and it is there, in the end, that we will find the room for a whole world."[1]

Richard Louv has ignited new concern and debate about this nature disconnect in his wildly popular book *Last Child in the Woods*, in which he argues that today's kids are suffering from "nature deficit disorder."[2] Too much time spent inside, too much time in front of the TV and computer, too little freedom to explore nature (and too little access to nature in new forms of development), and parental concerns about safety (the "bogeyman syndrome," as Louv calls it) are all contributing factors to this nature disconnect.

These concerns dovetail with health concerns about our overweight, sedentary children, but for me they represent an even more dire prospect of future generations of adults who don't viscerally or passionately care about nature, are little interested in its protection or restoration, and will miss out on the deeper life experiences that such natural experiences and connections can provide.

These trends, and these profound disconnects from nature in childhood and adulthood, suggest the time is ripe to revisit how we design and plan our communities and cities. There are many reasons to worry about our loss of intimate contact with nature, and they come together to create a compelling argument for a new vision of what cities could be. I draw from the theory and research associated with biophilia and argue that we need to reimagine cities as biophilic cities. A biophilic city is a city abundant with nature, a city that looks for opportunities to repair and restore and creatively insert nature wherever it can. It is an outdoor city, a physically active city, in which residents spend time enjoying the biological magic and wonder around them. In biophilic cities, residents care about nature and work on its behalf locally and globally.

The Power of Nature

That we need daily contact with nature to be healthy, productive individuals, and indeed have coevolved with nature, is a critical insight of Harvard myrmecologist and conservationist E. O. Wilson. Wilson popularized the term *biophilia* two decades ago to describe the extent to which humans are hardwired to need connection with nature and other forms of life. More specifically, Wilson describes it this way: "Biophilia . . . is the innately emotional affiliation of human beings to other living organisms. Innate means hereditary and hence part of ultimate human nature."[3]

To Wilson, biophilia is really a "complex of learning rules" developed over thousands of years of evolution and human–environment interaction: "For more than 99 percent of human history people have lived in hunter–gatherer bands totally and intimately involved with other organisms. During this period of deep history, and still further back they depended on an exact learned knowledge of crucial aspects of natural history. . . . In short, the brain evolved in a biocentric world, not a machine-regulated world. It would be therefore quite extraordinary to find that all learning rules related to that world have been erased in a few thousand years, even in the tiny minority of peoples who have existed for more than one or two generations in wholly urban environments."[4]

Stephen Kellert of Yale University reminds us that this natural inclination to affiliate with nature and the biological world constitutes a "weak genetic tendency whose full and functional development depends on sufficient experience, learning, and cultural support."[5] Biophilic sensibilities can atrophy, and society plays an important role in recognizing and nurturing them.

So we need nature in our lives; it is not optional but essential. Yet as the global population becomes ever more urban, ensuring that contact becomes more difficult. While architects and designers are beginning to incorporate biophilia into their work, planners and policymakers who think about cities have lagged behind. The subject at hand raises serious questions about what a city is or could be and what constitutes a livable, sustainable place. I believe there is a need to articulate a theory and practice of city planning that understands that cities and urban areas must be wild and "nature-ful." *Wildness,* in this book, refers to urban nature, which is inherently human impacted or influenced. Urban wildness is not wilderness as we have traditionally conceived it in environmental circles. It is not distant and pristine, defined by how little humans have used or impacted it, but nearby and nuanced; it is as much defined by its resilience and persistence in the face of urban pressures. It is the indomitable wind and weather, the plants that sprout and volunteer on degraded sites, the lichen and micro-organisms that inhabit and thrive on the façades of buildings, and the turkey vultures and red-tailed hawks that ply the airways and ride thermal currents high above urban buildings. *Wildness* in this book doesn't mean untouched or removed but instead refers to the many creatures and processes operating among us that are at once fascinating, complex, mysterious, and alive. In the urban epoch more than ever we need creative urban design and planning that makes nature the centerpiece, not an afterthought.

As Stephen Kellert notes, these are unusual times indeed when we actually have to defend and rationalize our need for contact with na-ture. The profound connection with the natural world has been for most of human history something pretty obvious. Yet today we seem entrenched in the view that we have been able, somehow, to overcome the need for nature, that we can "transcend" nature, perhaps even that we have evolved beyond needing nature.

The empirical evidence of the truth of biophilia, and of social, psy-chological, pedagogical, and other benefits from direct (and indirect) ex-posure to nature, is mounting and impressive. Some of the earliest work shows the healing power and recuperative benefits of nature. Roger Ulrich, of Texas A&M University, studied postoperative recovery for gall bladder patients in hospital rooms with views of trees and nature, compared with those with views of walls. Patients with the more natural views were found to recover more easily and quickly: "The patients with the tree view had shorter postoperative hospital stays, had fewer negative evaluative com-ments from nurses, took fewer moderate and strong analgesic doses, and had slightly lower scores for minor postsurgical complications."[6] These are not surprising results and have helped shift the design of hospitals and medical facilities in the direction of including healing gardens, natural daylight, and other green features.

The body of research confirming the power of nature continues to expand. Research shows the ability of nature to reduce stress, to enhance a positive mood, to improve cognitive skills and academic performance, and even to help in moderating the effects of ADHD, autism, and other child-hood illnesses. A recent study by the British mental health charity MIND compared the effects on mood of a walk in nature with a walk in a shop-ping mall.[7] The differences in the effects of these two walks are remarkable though not unexpected. The results show marked improvements in self-esteem following the nature walk (90% improved) but rather small improve-ments for those walking in the shopping center. Indeed, 44 percent of the indoor walkers actually reported a *decline* in self-esteem. Similarly, the out-

Figure 1.1 Canyons with San Diego Skyline in the background. Photo credit: Tim Beatley

door walk resulted in significant improvements in mood (six factors were measured: depression, anger, tension, confusion, fatigue, and vigor). The different mood effects are especially great with respect to tension. For the outdoor walk, 71 percent of participants reported a reduction in tension (and no increases), while for the indoor walk some 50 percent of the participants actually reported an *increase* in tension.

Hartig and his colleagues have undertaken a series of studies and experiments that bolster these findings, similarly demonstrating that views of nature and walks in natural settings can reduce mental fatigue, improve test performance, and improve mood (and more so than in urban settings without natural qualities).[8] "Views from indoors onto nature can support micro-restorative experiences that interrupt stress arousal or the depletion of attentional capacity. Similarly, when moving through the environment from one place to another, passage through a natural setting may provide a respite that, although brief, nonetheless interrupts a process of resource depletion. Frequent, brief restorative experiences may, over the long run, offer cumulative benefits."[9]

This is good news in that the nature in dense, compact cities may be found in smaller doses and in more discontinuous ways (a rooftop garden, an empty corner lot, a planted median) than in nonurban locations.

Biophilic urbanism must also strive, of course, for more intensive and protracted exposure to nature (further discussed below), but even the smaller green features we incorporate into cities will have a positive effect.

Few elixirs have the power and punch to heal and restore and rejuvenate the way that nature can. The power of biophilia suggests that everything that we design and build in the future should incorporate natural elements to a far greater extent—indoors and outdoors (and indeed the need to overcome these overly artificial distinctions), green neighborhoods, integrated parks and wild areas, not far away but ideally all around us.

Green Cities, Healthy Cities

Evidence suggests that the presence of green neighborhoods has broader and more pervasive impacts on health than we sometimes appreciate. In a national study involving more than ten thousand people in the Netherlands, researchers found significant and sizable relationships between green elements in living environments and higher levels of self-reported physical and mental health. As the authors conclude, "In a greener environment people report fewer symptoms and have better perceived general health. Also, people's mental health appears better."[10] The level of health was directly correlated to the level of greenness: "10% more greenspace in the living environment leads to a decrease in the number of symptoms that is comparable with a decrease in age by 5 years."[11]

A 2007 Danish study demonstrates the importance of access and proximity to parks and nearby greenspaces: These green features were found to be associated with lower stress levels and a lower likelihood of obesity.[12]

Studies suggest that green features help to draw us outside and propel us to live more physically active lives. Peter Schantz and his colleagues in Stockholm have demonstrated that green features correlate with decisions to walk or bike to work. Schantz refers to these green urban features as "pull factors for physical activity."[13] Leading more physically active lives outdoors will pay tremendous dividends to urbanites in good health. A 2009 survey of ten thousand residents of New York City, the most walkable city in the country, concludes that respondents who walk or bike daily are more likely, even controlling for income, to report being in good health, physically and mentally.[14]

Many other aspects of community and environmental health are quite effectively addressed through biophilic design and planning. Green urban features, such as trees and green rooftops, serve to address the urban heat island effect and to moderate and reduce urban heat; this has the potential to significantly reduce heat-related stress and illness in cities, something we must worry even more about as many American cities experience a significant rise in summer temperatures. There are, moreover, important air quality benefits from green features, another example of the secondary benefits of trees and urban nature. Trees and plantings on green rooftops, for instance, have been found to significantly reduce air pollutants such as sulfur dioxide and particulates.[15]

The nature and greenspaces around us also form an important community resource in times of trouble and stress. A 2009 survey by the Trust for Public Land, for instance, concludes that there has been a significant rise in the use of public parks as the national and global economy has soured.[16] Perhaps with unemployment on the rise a natural result is that individuals and families have more time to spend in such places, but this trend reinforces the very important role that outdoor nature can play in helping to buttress and buffer families in times of economic and social stress.

The Economics of Biophilia

Evidence suggests that there are very clear economic benefits to these green urban elements. A number of studies have shown that homes with trees, for instance, sell at premium compared with those without trees. A biophilic community is a place where residents can easily get outside, where walking, strolling, and meandering is permissible, indeed encouraged, and evidence suggests that these qualities now carry an economic premium. A 2009 study by CEO for Cities found that homes in more walkable environments carried a price premium of between $4,000 and $34,000 when compared with similar homes in other places.[17] Major urban greening projects, like the dramatic daylighting of four miles of the Cheonggycheon River through downtown Seoul, South Korea, which involved the removal of an elevated highway, serve to dramatically enhance the desirability and economic salability for the homes and neighborhoods nearby.[18]

New green urban elements and features are often rewarded in the marketplace and serve to stimulate new development and redevelopment. Recent examples include the High Line in New York City, the conversion of an elevated freight rail line into a new linear park, and Millennium Park in Chicago; both have stimulated new commercial and residential development, as clear amenity value and overall neighborhood enhancement

results from urban greening. The High Line has stimulated an estimated
$4 billion in private investment.[19]

Nature is a significant neighborhood asset and is seen as such by the
real estate market. And of course these green urban features, also known as
green infrastructure, provide cities with tremendous amenities and ecological services (economically valuable benefits that might otherwise have to
be provided through expensive technology and built projects), and though
frequently obscure and ambiguous (rarely do we calculate them), the economic or fair market value of these benefits is great. A recent study of
coastal wetlands concludes that the value of just the hurricane protection
they provide is an astounding $23 billion dollars per year.[20] A 2009 study
of the economic value created by New York's Central Park is a whopping
$1 billion a year (including millions of dollars of health benefits associated
with physical exercise).[21] Property with even a snippet of a view of the park
fetches astronomical real estate prices, but even greening the interstices and
sometimes forgotten spaces of the city can pay significant economic benefits. When the City of Chicago installed a green rooftop on its city hall,
there were rumors that building owners with apartments and spaces looking
down on the verdant rooftop were raising their rents.

Many of the biophilic urban elements described in this book provide undeniable and valuable services: They contain and manage stormwater and urban runoff, they provide shade and natural air conditioning in
hot weather, and they can produce potable water and even food for us to
eat. In my own home city of Charlottesville, Virginia, we enjoy a downtown
pedestrian mall with very large trees in the center. They serve to make outdoor eating and strolling possible and enjoyable, and by my occasional mea-
surements they are some ten degrees cooler on a hot summer day than other
less vegetated spaces in the city. Toronto has adopted a mandate (that came
into effect in 2010 for residential buildings) that requires the installation of
green rooftops for buildings over a certain size (any new development with
floorspace of more than 2,000 square meters has to devote between 20%
and 60% of its roof to vegetation). The environmental and even climate-
enhancing value is tremendous. A 2005 study of the potential impact of
greening rooftops in Toronto concluded that the space available is significant (some 5,000 hectares of roofs in the city greater than 350 square meters in size), and if green rooftops were installed, the city would experience
a reduction in ambient air temperatures of between 0.5 and 2.0 degrees
Celsius.[22]

The economic, environmental, and quality-of-life payoff is undeniable and considerable. Designing and planning for biophilia, even without the
deeper pleasures and meaning, makes economic and environmental sense.

Healing Urban Ills

Nature also has unusually potent power to heal broken human landscapes and to humanize and reinvigorate distressed cities and built environments. Recent efforts at greening through tree planting and new community gardens in urban neighborhoods in Detroit, Philadelphia, Cleveland, and other cities hard hit by the recession show the potential to restore community and hope at the same time that urban ecosystems are repaired. A nonprofit organization called The Greening of Detroit, for instance, undertakes a variety of urban greening projects from tree planting to building community gardens as a strategy for enhancing quality of life in some of Detroit's struggling neighborhoods. Partnering with other organizations, it supports the conversion of some of the city's sixty thousand vacant parcels into neighborhood-enhancing parks, play areas, and community gardens.[23] There are many other examples, from Sustainable South Bronx to Philadelphia Green, that show how essential urban nature and biophilic planning help to address the social and economic ills of distressed urban environments.

There are great inequities in the distribution of nature and green features in cities today, which we must be cognizant of and seek to overcome in the design of biophilic cities. In Los Angeles, parkland per capita for African American and Latino neighborhoods is dramatically lower, for instance, than for white neighborhoods.[24] And maintenance of parks and greenspaces varies, as well, by class and income. Efforts to expand and grow nature in cities have the potential to profoundly rectify these inequities. Restoring the natural qualities and ecology of the Los Angeles River, for instance, currently a concrete flood channel, has the potential to bring new nature into many neighborhoods in that city that need it desperately.

Environments rich with nature and natural experiences will help promote other important values. Exposure to nature, for instance, will likely help strengthen commitments to sustainability and living a more sustainable life. Survey data suggest that "nature-protective behaviors" (e.g., taking steps to protect nature such as signing a petition or recycling) are predicted by the emotional affinity for nature, in turn a function of the time and frequency of nature experiences.[25] Many of the actions and behaviors that we might imagine good citizens of a biophilic city undertaking, such as volunteering for stream restoration work or planting trees in one's neighborhood or serving as a citizen scientist collecting bird data or adding to the local natural history museum's plant collection, will deepen and strengthen bonds to place and community.[26] The nature around us, and the personal engagement with that nature, actually helps us, then, to become better environmentalists and citizens. If we are concerned about how to overcome the environmental apathy of our times, at both global and local scales, there can be no better way to do it than to ensure that urbanites are immersed in nature and actively involved in its restoration and stewardship.

It also appears that exposure to nature will actually help us become better human beings. Researchers at the University of Rochester have demonstrated through a series of clever experiments that people immersed in nature actually exhibit more generous behavior. The experiments compare the behaviors and attitudes of participants in experimental settings exposed to nature with those who were not (in one case participants are shown slides; in another the physical setting is manipulated by adding or taking away plants). Not surprisingly, across these experiments the researchers consistently found that participants exposed to nature (slides of nature rather than built environments, and lab settings full of plants) are much more likely to report so-called intrinsic aspirations (values that have inherent worth, such as intimacy or community, contrasted with extrinsic aspirations such as fame or wealth) and more likely to behave generously in a series of tasks involving the distribution of money.[27] Why this is so is not entirely clear, but these researchers suggest it is the result of a combination of enhancing personal autonomy and promoting feelings of closeness to nature. "Specifically, nature can bolster autonomy directly by affording stimulating sensations (e.g., environmental stimuli that are naturally interesting and personally satisfying and that facilitate orientation to the present . . . and opportunities to integrate experience by encouraging introspection and a coherent sense of self . . . and indirectly by presenting an alternative to the pressuring elements of everyday life."[28] These researchers continue, "In either case, nature affords individuals the chance to follow their interests and reduces pressures, fears, introjects, and social expectations."[29]

Nature helps us in caring about and connecting with the human communities of which we are part and perhaps ultimately stems from an evolutionary need for compassion, caring, and cooperation. Whatever the ultimate source, or psychological process or dynamic, nature seems to bring out the best in us.

Overcoming De-Natured Childhoods

Much of the current debate about the need for access to nature has focused on children (such as Richard Louv's *Last Child in the Woods*). Research confirms that children need to live their lives close to nature, with outdoor play as a central component.[30]

A 2010 Kaiser Family Foundation nationwide survey of media use by eight- to eighteen-year-olds found that these kids are spending 7.5 hours a day on average using media—television, video games, music, and the Internet. This is an astounding increase of an hour and seventeen minutes from the Kaiser study conducted five years ago. Most alarming is that the study found a correlation between heavy media use and poor grades and lower personal contentment. Those who use media heavily (16 or more hours a day) are "more likely to say they get into trouble a lot, are often sad or unhappy, and are often bored."[31] While the authors are cautious about concluding too much about causal effects, these correlations hold when other variables are controlled. These trends are not very encouraging and demonstrate both the sheer time commitment to media and the educational and deeper psychological impacts of such a life. There is little time for nature, it seems, but ever more need for its powers of engagement and wonder and meaning.

Much contemporary writing and commentary, and not a few parents looking back on their own childhoods, bemoan the decline in the freedom children once had to independently explore and investigate, to climb trees, and to build forts and tree houses. The ability for kids to climb trees, to play in nearby woods, and to walk and explore on the way to school has diminished inversely with our worries about traffic and crime

Figure 1.2 Vivid fungi in the city. Photo credit: Tim Beatley

and abductions. Many design professionals, this author included, now aspire to community design conditions that allow, indeed encourage, "free range kids." My colleague Peter Newman, at Curtin University in Australia, even boldly asserts that it is actually *feral* kids that we need. There are ways to design and plan this future, and biophilic cities offer some hope in this regard.

The freedom to flip over rocks looking for bugs or to dip one's feet in local streams, in endless and slow time, is important for getting to know, in a very hands-on way, the nature around us. Robert Pyle writes of the "extinction of experience" that occurs as availability of and access to natural areas diminishes. In Pyle's view, lack of personal contact with nature breeds alienation and in turn apathy about future protection and conservation of nature, in a kind of downward spiral, or "cycle of dis-affection."[32] "As cities and metastasizing suburbs forsake their natural diversity, and their citizens grow more removed from personal contact with nature, awareness and appreciation retreat. This breeds apathy toward environmental concerns and, inevitably, further degradation of the common habitat."[33]

An episode that occurred during a recent visit to one of our regional parks brought this home to me. Here, alongside the jungle gyms, slides, swings, and other typical play equipment was a fairly large pine tree. While I was watching over the play of my daughter, a policeman arrived at the tree, conveying a sense of urgency and seriousness about the young boy who was rather gleefully climbing and moving gracefully from one tree limb to another. Whose boy was this, he asked the group, and the boy's father, who had been playing catch nearby with his older son, spoke up: "He's a good climber and has never not been able to get down." The father was a bit incredulous (understandably so) at the very asking of the question. Someone had called the police, apparently concerned about the boy and fearing that he was lost (the exact motivations for the call were unclear) and in any event not being supervised by a parent. It brought home to me what the prevailing sense of parenting is—climbing trees, at least in this case, is dangerous fare and, if allowed, must be monitored closely and kept to a modest risk (don't climb higher than the first set of limbs!).

Sedentary, indoor lives represent a major health problem for both children and adults. The 2009 assessment of national trends by the Trust for America's Health found that obesity rates are rising in twenty-three states, and it raised special concerns about "obese baby boomers," for whom these sedentary lifestyles will serve to further compound the health and medical problems encountered later in life.[34] Some 65 percent of Americans are overweight, and the Centers for Disease Control and Prevention estimate the health care price tag of these sedentary trends to exceed $75 billion annually.

Recent studies show that a sizeable percentage of children are not getting the vitamin D their bodies need, in large part because they are not outdoors, not exposed to the sun. Some 70 percent of a sample of six thousand children and young adults were found to be deficient, with deficiency especially prevalent in children who spent four or more hours each day inside and watching television.[35]

Few have made a more compelling and eloquent plea for the importance of wonder in the natural world than Rachel Carson more than half a century ago. In her 1956 essay "Help Your Child to Wonder," she de - scribes the value and pleasures of exposing her young nephew to nature along the Maine coast: "If I had influence with the good fairy who is supposed to preside over the christening of all children I should ask that her gift to each child in the world be a sense of wonder so indestructible that it would last throughout life, as an unfailing antidote against the boredom and disenchantments of later years, the sterile preoccupation with things that are · artificial, the alienation from the sources of our strength."[36] Carson counsels looking at the sky, taking walks and uncovering and experiencing nature, even if (as parents) we are not able ourselves to identify a species or a constellation. It is about cultivating an awareness of the sights, sounds, and natural rhythms around us, paying attention and learning to see the mystery and beauty in everything around us.

And to Carson it is about developing a life skill and orientation, if you will, that will pay many dividends: "I am sure there is something much deeper, something lasting and significant. Those who dwell, as scientists or laymen, among the beauties and mysteries of the earth are never alone or weary of life. Whatever the vexations or concerns of their personal lives, their thoughts can find paths that lead to inner contentment and to renewed excitement in living. Those who contemplate the beauty of the earth find reserves of strength that will endure as long as life lasts."[37] "There is something infinitely healing," Carson says, "in the repeated refrains of nature—the assurance that dawn comes after night, and spring after winter."[38]

There is both systematic and anecdotal evidence showing how important family experiences in nature tend to be. Affinity for and love of nature are positively influenced by the amount and frequency of time spent in nature, and there is an extra and significant influence when this time is spent with members of one's family.[39] It makes complete sense, of course, as pleasant walks and outdoor time generate memories of place and environment and also of family. Parents, moreover, are in a unique position to convey both information about the surrounding nature and its emotional importance and value. Experience from Australia suggests that extended family members, grandparents in particular, are also a potent force in imparting love of and fascination with the natural world.[40]

Nature and the Wonder of Urban Living

Nature should not be an afterthought or viewed only in terms of the functional benefits (considerable as they are) it typically provides (managing stormwater, mediating air and water pollutants, addressing urban heat island effects, and so on).

We need wonder and awe in our lives, and nature has the potential to amaze us, stimulate us, and propel us forward to want to learn more about our world. The qualities of wonder and fascination, the ability to nurture deep personal connection and involvement, visceral engagement in something larger than and outside ourselves, offer the potential for meaning in life few other things can provide.

My landscape architecture colleague Beth Meyer argues that with matters of environment and sustainability we need also to emphasize the beauty and pleasure and enjoyment we derive. We often forget about the aesthetics or try to reduce them to monetary values. At the end of the day, watching that circling hawk or turkey vulture, walking or bicycling through an urban woods, harvesting and eating produce from one's garden, and listening to the sounds of katydids and tree frogs on a humid August evening are deeply pleasurable; they are the building blocks of a life enjoyed. We climb trees as kids because this is a fun and enjoyable thing to do, and as adults unfortunately we often forget these pleasures (and of course rarely climb trees!).

In our *Nature of Cities* documentary film we spent several stimulating days in Austin, Texas, filming the 1.5 million Mexican free-tailed bats that inhabit the underside of the city's Congress Avenue Bridge during the summer. People line up hours before nightfall to get a good look at the wondrous columns of bats emerging from beneath the bridge. Merlin Tuttle, founder of Bat Conservation International (BCI), dutifully recites the many environmental (and economic) benefits that these bats provide the city. For example, the bats eat millions of mosquitoes each day. But ultimately, the sight of thousands of bats flying off, in distinct columns that can be seen for several miles, is an immense and beautiful thing. It is the raw emotion and beauty of the natural world, a primordial spectacle unfolding against a backdrop of high-rise buildings and a human-dominated (at least we think) urban environment.

A deeper and fuller understanding of nature, of the biology and life cycles of plants and animals nearby, has the potential to profoundly reshape our notion of cities and our conception of the places in which we live. Jennifer Wolch, dean of the UC–Berkeley School of Environmental Design, has written of the concept of zoöpolis, an understanding of cities and communities as places where animals and people can co-occupy space, can *coexist*.[41] As Wolch says, "To allow for the emergence of an ethic, practice and politics of caring for animals and nature, we need to renaturalize cities and invite animals back in—and in the process re-enchant the city."[42] Paying attention to the animals and nature around us, educating about their presence and making room for them, and restoring and repairing urban habitats have the great potential to make cities magical. A fuller appreciation of and deeper caring for the animals and nature around us, then, can imbue cities and suburbs with new meaning—an "enchantedness," to paraphrase Wolch—creating places that are inherently shared by a fascinating and wondrous subset of the planet's biological diversity.

We need the design and planning goals of cities to include wonder and awe and fascination and an appreciation for the wildness that every city harbors. The incredible and abundant nature around us even in dense cities represents an important antidote to the boredom and sameness that otherwise characterizes much of our built form and lives.

Many Americans, I suspect, have great difficulty in even understanding that cities harbor or support much nature. The challenge for us in imagining and designing biophilic cities will be in shifting the perception, to appreciate that there is indeed nature all around. And as Kellert argues, it is the "local, everyday nature" we need. While places like Yellowstone and Yosemite are essential for many reasons (conservation of larger wildlife and biodiversity), we must overcome our perceptual bias that cities are biologically and biophilically impoverished places; quite the contrary is true.

Wilson and others have pondered whether the global loss of biodiversity impoverishes the human species and whether we are creating the conditions for a lonely existence. Hard-surfaced urban environments, barren and gray, often feel lonely due to the absence of not only people and active street life but also animals and other nonhuman life. We need these "others" to complete us, to fend off loneliness.

Concluding Thoughts

Biophilia suggests that there is an evolutionary and biological need for contact with nature, even when we have become very clever at believing we can live without it. Nature in our lives is not optional but essential. We need it for our emotional health and well-being, and we need it for planetary health as well. It is not a thing or a place that we periodically visit but a surrounding condition, an ideally ubiquitous context that delights, relaxes, soothes, replenishes, inspires, and uplifts us in our daily urban lives. It is all around us, and we live in it. Luckily, investments in green and nature-ful cities are good investments on many levels, and there are few more effective ways in which cities can be improved and the quality of lives of residents profoundly enhanced, while ecological footprints are reduced. Too often the green urban agenda forgets the "green," concentrating on energy efficiency and resource management (worthy and important subjects), for instance, to the neglect of the life-enhancing and wonder-expanding dimensions of nature itself.

Two

The Nature of (in) Cities

Several years ago an advertisement appeared in the real estate section of the *Washington Post*[1] promoting a new development: "The *NICE THING* about the city is that it eventually ENDS" (emphasis in original). The image juxtaposed sidewalks, a fire hydrant, and other essentially gray surfaces in the foreground (bad) with the bucolic images of forest and farm field in the distance (good). The implications were clear—if you want any meaningful exposure to nature, quickly exit the city. Unfortunately, this reflects the popular attitude toward cities and nature.

There are elements of truth to the sentiments expressed in this advertisement—there are in fact, too many bleak gray neighborhoods, too many cars, too much pavement—but the message is wrong in some profoundly significant ways. Cities are inherently complex ecosystems, nature is all around us in cities, and the extent of urban biodiversity is often quite considerable. The nature in cities is large and small, visible and hidden, intricate yet sweeping. It is amazing in its biological functioning, ever-present yet highly dynamic, and vastly underappreciated for its ubiquity in cities.

A biophilic city is a green city, a city with abundant nature and natural systems that are visible and accessible to urbanites. It is certainly about physical conditions and urban design—parks, green features, urban wildlife, walkable environments—but it is also about the spirit of a place, its emotional commitment and concern about nature and other forms of life, its interest in and curiosity about nature, which can be expressed in the budget priorities of a local government as well as in the lifestyles and life patterns of its citizens. In the next chapter, I discuss in more depth what a biophilic city entails.

There are many good reasons to learn more about and protect even the microscopic life around us, a biological storehouse of immense human value, of course, and wise sages from Aldo Leopold to Rachel Carson advise against the hubris of imperiling (or ignoring) even the most minute life-forms. Eric Chivian and Aaron Bernstein, of the Harvard Medical School, make a convincing argument in their important book *Sustaining Life* that conservation of biodiversity is highly connected to human health.[2] Loss of biodiversity, they rightly argue, is about losing a host of actual or potential benefits and services—from ecological services, to food production, to the production of new medicines, biodiversity is essential, not optional, to our lives and our health and to our continuing to flourish as a species.

In understanding the nature of cities it is necessary to think beyond our usual approach to visualizing or imagining space and place, and to understand that we can see nature everywhere in cities: it is above us, flying or floating by, it is below our feet in cracks in the pavement, or in the diverse microorganic life of soil and leaf litter. Nature reaches our senses, well beyond sight, in the sounds, smells, textures, and feelings of wind and sun. Understanding the natural history of a city helps us to see cities as ever-changing, ever-evolving palettes of life.

The Nature Above

Many things in cities take to the skies, and we should begin to understand the airspace above buildings, roads, and parks as life routes used by birds and bats and insects that spend at least some of their life in the air. It would be an interesting visual exercise to chart the paths and pathways of birds in a block or square kilometer of space over the course of day (it might look denser than the historic maps of hurricane tracks in a coastal state like Florida) and would give a visceral sense of the presence of these creatures (underappreciated, I think) in daily urban life. Seeing (and hearing) birds offers urban residents a series of daily delights, pleasant momentary mental escapes into another world, experienced on the way to the subway or on one's balcony on a Saturday morning.

Cities harbor an impressive diversity of birds, both residents and migrants, though many species are in decline in urban areas. In Chicago, 5–7 million birds, some 250 species, pass through the city during peak mi - gration times in fall and spring. The city sits smack-dab in the middle of the Mississippi Flyway, an amazing aerial superhighway that connects the Northern and Southern hemispheres. There are so many birds passing through that concerns about collisions with high-rise buildings have prompted the city to initiate a "lights out" campaign, aimed at turning off or dimming these disorienting lights. Studies by the Chicago Field Museum show that the program is effective in significantly reducing the mortality of migrating birds,[3] and although participation in the program is voluntary, companies and building owners are clearly motivated to care for the birds. And of course, there are other benefits, including reducing energy consumption and greenhouse gas emissions and, not least, saving money.

Toronto's lights-out program has an extensive advertising campaign with the tagline "Kill the lights, save the birds," which appears on subway and bus stops and even recycling bins. Toronto released a set of bird-friendly development guidelines in 2007 also voluntary, that recommend a number of ways in which new buildings in the city can be designed to reduce collisions, including using glass with "visual markers and muting reflections"; using awnings, sunshades, and downward-angled glass to reduce reflections; minimizing unnecessary exterior decorative lighting; and designing buildings so that task lighting can be used during the evening.[4]

Perhaps most unusual, the City of Toronto has funded the development of a "bird-friendly rating system" for new buildings. As in other green-building rating systems, a building can accumulate a series of points for bird-friendly design elements, allowing it to qualify for one of three certification levels: Minimum, Preferred, and Excellent.[5] Once certified, builders and developers who meet the standards receive recognition from the city and are able to market their buildings as "bird-friendly." In Toronto, an NGO called FLAP (Fatal Light Awareness Program) has spearheaded these efforts to raise awareness of the need for more bird-friendly buildings. In 2007 FLAP organized an eye-catching exhibit of the more than 2,500 birds that were killed by flying into buildings and then collected by the group. It was a visible demonstration of both the diversity and the numbers of birds passing through the city and the urban perils faced along the way.[6]

Urban birding is a cherished hobby of many urbanites, a pursuit that takes people outside and places them in contact with the life around them. New York City's Central Park, for instance, is a perhaps unexpected epicenter for birding. There are an estimated 270 species of birds in Central Park, none more famous than the red-tailed hawks. Pale Male, a resident male red-tailed hawk who was made a celebrity through books and a PBS documentary, is avidly watched by residents and visitors alike. On a frigid March day, we found a group of Japanese tourists, mixed with strolling New Yorkers, lined up to get a glimpse through a telescope of Pale Male and his current mate, nesting on the ledge of a rather expensive apartment building along Park Avenue. Hawks and peregrine falcons can be found in many other places around the city and not necessarily in traditional parks. For instance, we found a pair of red-tailed hawks nesting high up in the Unisphere, the distinctive metal globe built for the 1964–65 World's Fair, in Flushing Meadows, Queens.

Figure 2.1 Peregrine falcon, the world's fastest animal.

Peregrine falcons have also returned to New York City, or more accurately have been reintroduced. The first pairs were introduced in the early 1980s, part of a larger effort to recover this species, and today there are more than thirty nesting pairs in the city. The dense city is in many ways quite suited to peregrine falcons. They have abundant food in the form of both resident birds and migrating ones, and the high-rise Manhattan buildings are not unlike the peregrine cliff habitat that provides a very good vantage for hunting. If you are lucky, you might witness a truly remarkable and wild act in a city: "The falcon will dive down onto its prey at speeds ranging from 99 to 273 miles per hour. . . . A City bridge or skyscraper provides a great deal of open air space and a unique perch for hunting."[7] Peregrine falcons are the fastest birds on Earth, indeed the fastest animals, and it is remarkable that they can be found in cities. It is not commonly realized that such speed may be seen on one's walk to the market or subway, and one need not travel to the African savanna to watch running cheetahs.

For several years downtown office workers in Richmond, Virginia, have been captivated by the aerial antics and parenting escapades of nesting peregrine falcons. One worker with a window view says, "I see them every day. . . . It's great to have such wonderful entertainment while I'm working!"[8] A falcon recovery effort is being spearheaded by the Center for Conservation Biology at the College of William and Mary. One unique aspect is the use of video webcams at each of the nesting sites, including the downtown site, so anyone can log on to see the peregrines. Many residents of Richmond who don't have the same visual access as the worker quoted above are avidly following the birds through the Internet (www.dgif .virginia.gov/falconcam2008/). And these efforts help to expand the base of political and popular support for such conservation efforts. Conservation is not to be viewed as simply something that trained scientists and professional resource managers do in faraway places. Rather, it has very local relevance and, through these efforts, clear connections to where people live and work.

Cities compete quite impressively with many supposed more natural settings in nonurban areas when it comes to birds and bird counts. Several years ago San Francisco came in second in the America's Birdiest City Competition, a contest to see how many different species could be counted in a single weekend. The city lost to the decidedly nonurban Dauphin Island, Alabama, but not by much, and it racked up an impressive 178 bird species.[9] San Francisco boasts a remarkable diversity of natural habitats and is home to nearly 400 bird species at some point during the year, a result in part of its critical position along the Pacific Flyway. About half the bird species in North America can be seen within the borders of this highly developed city.

The higher reaches of our cities—the rooftops and façades—also harbor nature, sometimes by design and sometimes by accident and natural volunteerism. New forms of nature are being created in cities all over the nation in the form of ecological rooftops and rooftop gardens, hosting grasses and sedums, which are increasingly found (over time and with the right design elements) to harbor great diversity in terms of invertebrates, birds, and plant life. We know, for instance, that butterfly species will visit rooftops on high-rise structures and that food, for humans and nature alike, can be grown there as well.

A visit to the Green Roofs Research Center, in Malmö, Sweden, shows the extent of possibilities—here they have planted and monitor hundreds of green roof test plots, testing different plant and soil combinations. Some of these plots are for so-called brown rooftops—places in the urban environments (there are many) where plants can be used to restore and even take up pollutants in highly contaminated and degraded settings (phytoremediation). And the Malmö center's immense research rooftop also shows the potential of different, sometimes surprising delivery methods. As Trevor Graham, who runs many of the center's green city efforts, explains, their standard green roof is made from recycled polyurethane car seats, and in several places there are small mounted frames, with sedum growing vertically, showing the potential for a kind of natural artwork suitable for hanging in one's living room! These new forms of nature are catching on and are now encouraged and in some places mandated by codes—and we will see more of this happening in every city around the world. New creative developments in cities—such as Via Verde (the green way), a 200-unit complex of affordable housing planned for a 1.5-acre site in the South Bronx of New York—will find many ways to insert and grow nature. In this case, the nature takes the form of a connected multifunctional garden "that begins at street-level as a courtyard and plaza, and spirals upward through a series of programmed, south-facing roof gardens that end in a sky terrace."[10] Increasingly, we will understand rooftops, courtyards, and façades in cities as places to cultivate nature.

Urban trees are another important form of nature in cities. We know now that there is a often a great diversity of life to be found at the tops of trees in the form of lichens, fungi, and mosses, many with unusual and little-understood life histories and biology. Richard Preston documents the tales of some of the more daring of the redwood tree climbers in a quest to understand this canopy life in his *New York Times* best seller *The Wild Trees*. These aerial botanists find amazing numbers of mosses and lichens, key parts of a canopy ecosystem few others have explored.[11]

Lichens are perhaps one of the least-understood and least-appreciated forms of nature but some of the most unusual and wildest occupants of cities. Found on rocky outcrops and stones, even on gravestones in urban cemeteries, they are most often found on the bark and limbs of trees. There are more than 3,600 different species of lichen in North America alone, many found in and around cities.[12]

There are few things in the city, or anywhere, as wild and primordial as lichens, and their biology and chemistry are not clearly understood. Lichens are in fact the merging of two life-forms—a fungus and, usually, an alga—that survive through mutual coexistence. The alga is a symbiont in this partnership, providing through photosynthesis the nutrients the fungus needs to live. Sometimes the symbiont is a cyanobacterium, as in the case of lettuce longwurt (*Lobaria oregano*), which incredibly pulls nitrogen directly from the air and is a source of natural fertilizer for trees. The chemistry of lichens is complex, with an estimated 1,000 compounds produced by them, some thought to be promising human antibiotics.[13]

Some studies suggest a remarkable diversity of lichen in cities. A recent study of lichens in Singapore concluded there were more than three hundred species in that city. It appears that similar levels of lichen flora can be found in other cities, such as Berlin and Hong Kong, for example.[14] High sulfur dioxide levels in cities have kept the numbers of lichen down in the past, but with improvements in air quality lichens seem to be on the rebound in many urban settings. The Field Studies Centre (FSC) in the UK has now published a set of guides to urban lichens, a recognition that in many cities in that country there has been remarkable rebound of this form of urban nature.[15]

Even more biodiversity can be found on the lichens and mosses living on tree branches. One very unique creature likely to be found on a lichen sample is the so-called water bear (sometimes even more charmingly called a moss piglet). About a millimeter in size, they are just out of the range of the naked eye, and few people have seen them or even know of their existence. They belong to a unique phylum of invertebrates called Tardigrada. They are quite unusual looking—four pairs of limbs, with claws, looking not unlike a microscopic version of a dugong or manatee. They lumber along slowly, in a bearlike fashion, hence the name. Their most remarkable characteristic is their ability to profoundly change in response to harsh environmental conditions. In particular, they can induce a kind of hibernation, a form of cryptobiosis in which they virtually dry up and desiccate.[16] Called anhydrobiosis, it results in an "almost complete loss of body water and the animal can stay in this state for an extended period of time."[17] Contracting and infolding its body, it does not seem to be alive, but even a hundred years later it can regenerate through rehydration. "The dry organisms may remain in this unique living state . . . for decades or perhaps centuries under favorable conditions. When water becomes available, they rapidly swell and resume active life."[18] What a remarkable creature to imagine inhabiting the branches of the trees in our urban and suburban neighborhoods!

We may learn much of practical value from the amazing biology of tardigrades, and already lichens, on which water bears are frequently found, are commonly used as bioindicators in urban environments. If lichens and water bears do not do well in cities, it is quite likely that human health is similarly impacted. And there is no clearer refutation of the belief that there are no more species left to discover than the story offered by Tardigrades. New species are being found and described all over the world, from Russia to Syria to the Great Smoky Mountains of North Carolina.[19] More fundamentally, I believe our lives are the richer for knowing about water bears, and a little bit of the mystery and intrigue of the life of this invertebrate rub off on our own in the process. And our knowing that all around us in cities there is abundant, fascinating life imbues these spaces and habitats with a kind of new color, a different mental map that says at once

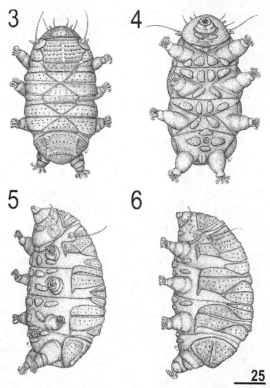

Figure 2.2 Water bears. Image credit: Reinhardt Møbjerg Kristensen and Birgitte Rubæk

we are not alone and that spaces that might at first seem vacant or empty are indeed not.

Even the more ephemeral occupants of the airspace above cities, notably clouds, can be found to harbor and sustain life. Our understanding of the biological dimensions of clouds has significantly increased in recent years. The usual image of clouds as inanimate phenomena is incorrect; they might more aptly be described as floating coral reefs, teeming with bacteria and other microorganisms. Several new scientific studies published in 2009 show the rich biology of clouds.[20] And these biological particulates—bacteria, fungi, algal material—are an important part of how a cloud produces rain and ice, which climatologists call *nucleators*. Our understanding is quite limited of so many things in nature, but the more we know about the biological or chemical complexity of, in this case, clouds, the greater the wonder coefficient.

The night sky is yet another form of wildness derived from an upward glance, though viewing the Milky Way, at least with the naked eye, is difficult to impossible from many urban locations because of modern light pollution. Viewing the phases of the moon is another urban and suburban delight, and there are few things more enjoyable than walking, hiking, or jogging on the evening of a full moon. Many communities are now committed to savoring and protecting such nature experiences, and many of the efforts to reduce or mute the often excessive lighting of buildings also help in protecting views of our night sky. A number of cities have adopted dark sky ordinances and lighting standards, and some have even become certified "dark sky communities," an initiative of the International Dark Sky Association.[21]

The Nature All Around

The spaces and habitats that occupy the city from ground to sky are in many ways the most familiar and the most noticeable to us.

Trees represent some of the most obvious forms of nature around us in cities—not simply the tips of the upper branches but the parts that are visually and tactilely accessible to us. Many city dwellers are rightly tree huggers and tree lovers. Some of the oldest and most impressive trees can be found in places like New York City, which has at least four groves of ancient trees, much older than most trees and forests found outside of the metropolitan area. It is counterintuitive perhaps, but as Mike Feller, the chief ecologist for New York's parks department, explained to me, the high degree of agricultural land use and extensive land clearance outside the cities strip much of the floral diversity. In this way cities serve as biological refuges. In many places, of course, new development within cities and at the urbanizing edge is leading to the loss of trees and tree cover, moving cities in the wrong direction. We need to protect what we have, as well as replace and add to the stock of trees in cities.

One of these floral wonders—an ancient tulip poplar tree—can be found in Queens, not far from Alley Pond Park, and I visited the tree with Mike Feller. This tulip tree, as *Liriodendron tulipifera* is commonly called, is a whopping 134 feet tall and an estimated 450 years old, likely the oldest living thing in the city. Affectionately referred to as the Queens Giant, it stands not far from the roar of traffic and for the most part is not widely appreciated—and there is controversy about whether it is adequately protected. But this magnificent tree is a time portal, linking us to the city's early settlement history and to a time before the Europeans arrived.[22]

Trees even older than the Queens Giant exist in the center of Stockholm, Sweden, where large ancient oaks are found a stone's throw away from the city's dense urban center. Here people like to talk about the thousand-year life span of these distinctive trees—they grow for five hundred years and then take another five hundred years to die and decompose. Many of these ancient oaks can be found in the city's large and unique EkoPark, a 27-square-kilometer area made up of natural and cultural landscapes, pastureland and nature, forests and archipelago, in the center of this metropolitan area. The mosaic of nature here is remarkable: "alder fens, spruce woods, shoreline forest, open meadows, and wooded pastures with very large ancient trees. There is also great biodiversity, with over 800 wild species of flowering plant and at least 100 species of nesting bird."[23] And it is the dying and decomposing of these oak trees that turns out to be an important element of preserving biodiversity—many endangered invertebrates depend upon that decomposition for life. "In the spring, carpets of wood anemone blossom amongst the oaks, while stock doves and tawny owls nest in the hollows of the oldest trees."[24]

Alley Pond Park, in Queens, is another example of a significant ecosystem and habitat in the city. It contains a system of remnant "kettle ponds," formed by the Minnesota Ice Sheet (this was the southern end of the glacier), which "dropped the boulders that sit on the hillsides of the southern end of the park and left buried chunks of ice that melted and formed the ponds."[25] Alley Pond is one of forty-eight sites in the Forever Wild program of the New York City Department of Parks and Recreation, which strives to protect ecologically rich land in New York City. Together the designated lands include almost nine thousand acres in five boroughs and represent a remarkable diversity of natural communities and habitat.[26]

Not far from Alley Pond is Jamaica Bay Wildlife Refuge, more than ninety-one hundred acres of salt marshes, mudflats, and maritime forests—a unique unit of the larger Gateway National Recreation Area. It is a diverse and wild refuge abutting Queens and Brooklyn, on the edge of the nation's densest city. Under threat from sea level rise and other pressures (the refuge has seen a significant reduction in marsh area since the 1950s, for instance), it is still an important site of respite and recreation and is easily reachable by train and bus from Manhattan (and also by bike and, from some locations, even by kayak). It is a significant stopover point for migratory birds on the Eastern Flyway, with some 331 species recorded (almost half of the species found in North America).[27]

Every city can and must find better ways to acknowledge, design within, and profoundly connect with the unique physical and ecological contexts in which they sit. Often the underlying topography, for instance, has been forgotten even through it likely shaped the city and region. In

some western cities like San Diego, which is defined by hundreds of surrounding canyons, these natural features are either forgotten or ignored,
or worse, actively destroyed and degraded.

Fortunately the last several years have witnessed new efforts on
the part of some local groups in San Diego to raise appreciation of these
canyons and even link what remains of them into a San Diego Regional
Canyonlands park. In March 2006, a provocative white paper further advocating and fleshing out the idea was released by the volunteer-led group San
Diego Civic Solutions. While a short paper, the vision is a compelling one
and sets out in text and renderings some of the main design ideas—limiting
encroachment of development, increasing access (visual and physical) and
connection, as through walking trails, designed in ways that discourage the
"blocking-off" of canyons. San Diego's canyons can, as the white paper argues, provide emotional and psychological benefits, can be places where
children learn about nature, and can be important elements in the region's
strategy for protecting biodiversity.[28] While few tangible steps have yet been
taken, this vision has helped to stimulate new interest in this immense local
ecology.

Many groups in the city are working hard to raise awareness of the
canyons, to organize cleanup and restoration work, and in some cases to
repel city projects that would damage or destroy canyons. The Sierra Club's
Canyons Campaign is helping to start and support some forty Friends of
the Canyons groups. Friends of Rose Canyon, one of the largest with about
twelve hundred members, is made up of people who care about and go to
bat for this amazing canyon. And there is much to do, including vigilantly
defending the canyons from various proposed encroachments, such as an in-
sane proposal to build a road directly through and across Rose Canyon.

The female bobcat that resides in Rose Canyon is certainly a source
of pride to residents there. We filmed a segment of *The Nature of Cities* in
Rose Canyon early one morning, following two women on an urban tracking session looking for signs of wildlife, including the elusive bobcat, by
searching for paw prints, scat remains, and other evidence of the movements
and life of animals in this canyon. For several hours we looked carefully at
every wet patch of mud, every broken branch, and every errant bird feather
that might indicate the recent presence of life. At one point in following
these women (this alone was a major feat), we heard yelps of joy as one
of the trackers indicated having found a dead bird, very recent prey for the
bobcat, the ultimate tracking prize on that day. Remarkably, these tracking experiences were all within a short distance of downtown San Diego,
with the sights and sounds of the city all around us (even a fast-moving
commuter train).

Figure 2.3 Bobcat, in Rose Canyon, San Diego.

One of the more interesting initiatives of the canyon campaign has been "Kids in Canyons," a program bringing elementary students to visit and learn about the canyons, run in collaboration with the nonprofit group Aquatic Adventures. Kids are guided through canyons, learn about the flora and fauna there, and in some cases help to do some cleanup and planting. One day we followed a group of students from a nearby elementary school as they learned about the natural habitat of the canyons. Most striking was the fact that although the elementary school itself was perched on the edge of this canyon, which was essentially around the corner and behind the school, the canyon itself might as well have been in another city. The school offered little or no programming in which the canyon figured, and indeed the canyon was seen (by kids and adults alike) as a dangerous place to be avoided rather than celebrated. Once in the canyon the students learned much about nature and the unique canyons of this city, and their negative impressions melted away.

E. O. Wilson, in his beautiful book *The Creation,* argues that we need to foster this wonder and fascination at an early age. Looking at and discovering the things around them is an ideal activity for kids. I agree with him that encouraging the natural impulses kids have to collect things from

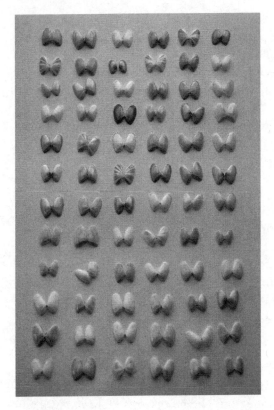

Figure 2.4 Coquina shells, collected off the Florida's gulf coast. Photo credit: Tim Beatley

nature is one step. I recall the delight my two young daughters experienced in collecting coquina shells in the sandbars off Sanibel Island, with the skyline of the city of Ft. Myers in the background. Coquina (*Donax variabilis*) show a remarkable diversity of color in their shells—purple, pink, blue, brown, seemingly every color and shade and design represented in nature. Collecting them takes a degree of delicate strategy in order to preserve the two halves in their attached form. This allows the mounting of the shells later, like so many butterflies, on paper or in a frame. The process of collecting coquina responds to several different values—for kids, of course, it is fun and involves running, diving, extruding handfuls of sand, and gleeful delight about what is discovered. There is a kind of hidden treasure, and one is never sure about what gem will be uncovered. It focuses the attention on the beauty and detail of nature—as the shells are washed, the true colors are uncovered. And there is much to be said for any family activity that keeps kids outdoors, hands and feet immersed in the natural world.

In San Francisco, a newly formed community group called Nature in the City has already produced a map of the parks and remnant patches of nature in that city, and the tally is surprising: gray foxes, alligator lizards, mission blue butterflies, and California quail (some endangered, many plentiful), amid some dozen native plant communities and natural areas within the city.[29] As Peter Brastow, founder of the organization, declares, this city is "resplendent with biodiversity and scenic natural areas."[30]

There are many small patches of green, of course, as San Francisco is already heavily built-out, but there are large tracts as well, notably Golden Gate Park, the Presidio, and Glen Canyon Park. Golden Gate Recreation Area is an astounding seventy-five thousand acres, so there is more green and nature here than perhaps is appreciated, and of course the city is also surrounded by blue nature in the form of the Pacific Ocean and the San Francisco Bay.

In the U.S. Midwest, there remain significant amounts of native prairie and other remnants of pre-European settlement. In the late 1990s, a group of environmental and other organizations joined together to form the Chicago Wilderness Coalition, with the goal of partnering to save, restore, and educate about the nature in this region. This alliance of now more than two hundred diverse organizations has put forth a powerful image of a biologically rich urban region, some 250,000 acres of land already protected in parks and natural areas and comprised of globally important natural communities, including "tallgrass prairie, oak woodlands, oak savannas, sedge meadows, marshes, bogs and fens."[31] The group has already prepared a *Biodiversity Atlas*[32] of the region and the first (and only) *Biodiversity Recovery Plan*[33] ever prepared for an urban region. The moniker of "Chicago Wilderness" is itself a clever attention-getter—to many an unlikely joining of these two words but a clear signal that there is much that is wild and primordial and natural amid the cars and buildings (see www.chicagowilderness.org).

In the Kansas City metro area, while little of the pre-European landscape remains, there is remarkably unique nature close at hand. An organization called Kansas City WildLands was formed in 2000 to watch over and to help repair this landscape. Larry Rizzo, one of the founders of WildLands and a biologist for the Missouri Department of Conservation, has written a useful guide[34] to Kansas City wildlands, which include a number of parks and natural areas in or near the city, drawing attention to what remains. These urban wildlands include bottomland hardwoods, prairies and open woodlands and savannas, and a remarkable diversity of life. Glades, for instance—rocky openings in the forest—along the Blue River are home to many wildflowers and birds, wild turkeys, and even scorpions. Remnant patches of prairie in the region harbor remarkable biodiversity: Kill Creek Prairie contains some two hundred species of plants, including the federally threatened Meade's milkweed, and perhaps an astounding thousand species of beetles.[35] All of this is within a few miles of downtown Kansas City, Missouri.

Some of the wildness in cities is large and obvious, as in the case of cities with a large visible mammal population that lives and moves in close proximity to urbanites. The city of Anchorage, Alaska, is one of the more dramatic examples of this in North America. There is remarkable wildlife within its borders, including as many as a thousand moose in winter, three hundred black bears, and sixty-five brown bears.[36] Visceral and direct contact with this nature is facilitated through the city's extensive 400-mile network of urban trails. The trail network offers diverse ways to enjoy the city's nature through all seasons of the year (hiking, biking, trails for cross-country skiing in winter, even dog-mushing trails).[37]

Very near to the city is Chugach State Park (the country's third-largest state park), a half-million acres of wildlands that are home to even more wildlife, including Dall sheep and mountain goats. There are also several packs of wolves in the metro area. Residents of Anchorage appear to be proud of the extent of the wildlife in and around their community and seem to understand its unique contribution to a sense of place. In a survey of attitudes about the city's wildlife, 87 percent agreed with the statement, "While moose cause some problems, they make life in Anchorage seem interesting and special."[38]

Urbanites in many eastern U.S. cities are now discovering that coyotes have moved into their neighborhoods, offering an unusual new degree of wildness, though not without some consternation about the safety of children and pets. The fears are largely unfounded and easily dispelled with a little education. Coyotes are not a threat to humans, and their diet consists primarily of small rodents, plants, and berries, and rarely the family cat.[39] Known to Native Americans as "God's Dog," the coyote has now even become a resident of the nation's capital, first sighted in Rock Creek Park in 2004. An estimated four thousand to seven thousand coyotes now live within the city limits of Los Angeles.[40] For many, an early morning sighting of a coyote is a magical gift and visceral evidence of the resiliency of nature and wildness.

Perhaps we need to look for ways to tap into the fun of looking for and finding things in nature at a community or collective level. One powerful process of this sort is the BioBlitz (or bioblitz), a 24-hour intensive search for all of the biodiversity, large and small, in a defined space or area, often a public park. BioBlitzes have been undertaken all over the world and have both a scientific and educational function. And sometimes they even result

Figure 2.5 Kids manning the nighttime moth collection station at the Balboa Park BioBlitz, San Diego, California. Photo credit: Tim Beatley

in discovery of new species (such as the new species of centipede, *Nannarup hoffmani,* discovered in New York's Central Park).

The potential of a BioBlitz was brought home vividly to me last year as I watched (and filmed) one of these searches unfolding over a day and night in San Diego. Organized by the San Diego Museum of Natural History and focused on recording the biodiversity of Balboa Park, the evening directly involved kids. There was an opportunity for kids to spend the night at the museum, which many did, immersing themselves in the science and fun of this event. Several nighttime observation stations were set up, and especially entertaining was the moth station. Scientists from the museum draped a white sheet over several dangling lights, in an effort (largely successful) to attract moths. Many moths appeared that evening, and between the "oohs" and "ahhs" the kids learned a great deal, I think, about the biology of these species. Perhaps the most important benefit was the fostering of curiosity and fascination and the mystery the evening holds for what it will bring in the form of unusual-looking fauna. Moths impressed me that evening with their ability to evoke a sense of mystery and magic. When they hear that almost ten thousand different species of moths can be found in North America, kids and adults alike are amazed.

The tally from that day and night in San Diego was impressive— more than a thousand species were recorded at Balboa Park. I came away appreciating how valuable such a process might be in service of community planning. The BioBlitz should be viewed as a useful source of information and insight about patterns of biodiversity in a community, and it is certainly helpful (if not essential) in developing a community plan that takes adequate account of nature and environment. Organizing one or more BioBlitzes as part of the community planning process would at once give visibility and importance to a process sometimes lacking in excitement or perceived relevance. Making the connection for residents between policies and actions in a plan and the fascinating and wondrous nature and life all around would be a positive thing. The BioBlitz helps to foster community—it is a biological block party, if you will.

The Nature Below

There is also much nature below—underfoot, underground, and underwater—in and around our cities. Much of this wondrous life in and around cities is hidden from view, and finding effective ways to highlight and make it visible is a major challenge for planners and designers.

In many American cities the biodiversity is aquatic and sometimes offshore, as in Seattle, which has abundant and wondrous life in the close-by depths of the bay and sound. Much of the biodiversity of King County, in which the city of Seattle lies, is found in the deep subtidal habitat of Puget Sound, in some places almost nine hundred feet below the surface and including "over 500 benthic and 50 pelagic invertebrates."[41] And while some, such as the king crab, are known and recognizable to residents, many remain unknown. That the Seattle metro region is also home to such unique marine critters as the giant Pacific octopus and giant acorn barnacle suggests a wildness and mystery very close at hand. The region's marine mammals get a bit more attention and visibility, including killer whales, which are now on the federally endangered species list.

Underfoot the diversity in cities is quite impressive: Fifty-one species of ants were recently categorized in the city of Philadelphia, for instance, enough to make any urban myrmecologist proud. San Francisco harbors nineteen species of ants and sixty different species of native bees (though we certainly hope they are found hovering near the surface and not underfoot as we walk through the city).[42]

One of my favorite examples of how the presence of these fascinating co-occupants of cities has been made more visible can be seen in the work of Walter Tschinkel, a Florida State University entomologist. Tschin - kel uses orthodontic plaster to make casts of subterranean ant nests and to

Figure 2.6 Giant Pacific octopus, a nearby underwater resident in Seattle, Washington.

render visible the nest architecture of species like the Florida harvester ant (*Pogonomyrmex badius*).[43] Reassembled as single, connected plaster models showing the shafts and chambers of these nests, they are, in Tschinkel's words, "undeniably spectacular." Tschinkel's research has already generated new knowledge about the biology of these ants (that there is a "vertical social structure by worker age and life stage"), but the functions of this elaborate nest architecture are mostly unknown. Nevertheless, the plaster casts—shafts 12 meters long, connecting some 135 different chambers— lend a sense of awe to ant biology that few of us are familiar with.

The work of scientists like Walter Tschinkel provides us with un- usual windows into the natural world but also has the potential to teach us important design lessons from nature. Biomimicry suggests that we tap into the wisdom of the natural world and learn from the millennia of evolution- ary trial and error when designing and planning. Office buildings have been designed based on the cooling principles found in the design of African termite mounds, for instance, and scientists at the Max Planck Institute in Germany are designing new adhesive materials based on the dense network of "mushroom shaped micro-hairs" found on the soles of insects.[44] Nature is fascinating and wondrous but may also hold creative and unimaginable design solutions to many of our most pressing social and environmental (and urban) challenges.

E. O. Wilson, in *The Creation*, calls attention to the amazing bio-diversity underfoot by referring to these areas as "micro-wildernesses." He seeks to muster our collective fascination at what exists there: "Each cubic meter of soil and humus within it is a world swarming with hundreds of thousands of such creatures, representing hundreds of species. With them are even greater numbers and diversity of microbes. In one gram of soil, less than a handful, live on the order of ten billion bacteria belonging to as many as six thousand species."[45] Wilson is an entomologist and an un-abashed proponent of paying more attention to the smaller, less obvious or visually dramatic things in the world. "More respect is due the little things that run the world."[46]

The biodiversity below is sometimes at the surface and can add much to the vitality and charm of the city. Such has been the case for the sea lions that several years ago arrived at Pier 39 in San Francisco. Origi-nally viewed as a nuisance, they have become a tourist attraction and a con-venient point of education about marine life. Staff of the Marine Mammal Center are present at the pier and use the sea lions as an opportunity to talk with visitors about this marine mammal and marine ecology. Recently, the sea lions disappeared (mysteriously) from the pier, setting in motion angst and disappointment on the part of many city residents who had become accustomed to seeing them and enjoying their presence. Finally in the spring of 2010, the sea lions began returning (from where is not clear), and a sigh of relief could be felt as residents monitored the action from a web-cam pointed at the pier. The story of San Francisco sea lions shows how viscerally engaged and caring and concerned residents of a major city can become when given the chance and how economically valuable such otherwise hidden life can be.

There are often a number of small mammals to watch for at ground level, and in many western American cities, these include prairie dogs. Last year I found myself sitting on the edge of a fence in Boulder, Colorado, watching a colony of black-tailed prairie dogs go about daily life, ever vigi-lant of my presence and occasionally issuing their characteristic warning barks. For me it was a visceral demonstration of the therapeutic and mes-merizing impact of nature, the fact that time essentially stood still in those moments of observation, a brief emotional respite in the course of my urban day. These prairie dogs are generally not doing well and are on the verge of being listed under the federal Endangered Species Act. Their presence in the urban and suburban areas of Denver suggests the positive role that cities might play as biological safe spots, and of course a need to contain the low-density suburban sprawl that is threatening many of these colonies. What is especially interesting to see are the ways in which these black-tailed prairie dogs have already adapted to their urban settings. As biologist Seth Magle notes, their colonies have become denser, given the more limited space available, and they exhibit new forms of adaptive behavior, what Magle refers to as "street smarts," including climbing shrubs for food and even swimming, behaviors quite uncommon in rural colonies.[47] Nature in cities often meets us halfway.

Multisensory Nature and the Enveloping Natural World

Experiencing nature in cities is as much about hearing, smelling, and feeling as it is about seeing. Touch and feel are often underappreciated as essential ways we experience nature around us. As brain scientist Jill Bolte Taylor notes, human skin is the largest of our sensory organs and intricately designed to sense and capture the feelings and sensations as we walk through a park or along a street. She explains that our skin is "stippled with very specific sensory receptors designed to experience pressure, vibration, light touch, pain, or temperature. These receptors are precise in the type of stimulation they perceive such that only cold stimulation can be perceived by cold sensory receptors. Because of this specificity, our skin is a finely mapped surface of sensory reception."[48] The entire body has evolved, it seems, to have fine receptors of the many earthly sensory signals sent our way.

The biophilic qualities of cities include, for many of us, the feelings associated with changing daily and seasonal climate, the gentle and not-so-gentle breezes that strike our faces as we move outside. In some cities these breezes are valued and celebrated. Freiburg and other German cities map and protect the wind corridors that come down from the Black Forest and prevent the construction of buildings that would interrupt or block these replenishing flows. These winds provide the cooling and rejuvenating fresh air for the city, sending away pollutants and fostering an awareness of climate.

In what other ways could we design and plan American communities with greater sensitivity to weather and climate? How could weather

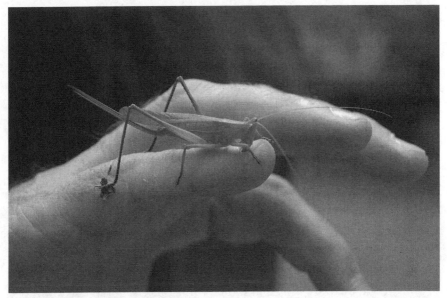

Figure 2.7 A katydid, one of the many producers of the lovely sounds that inhabit cities. Photo credit: Tim Beatley

and climatic conditions become aspects of places and regions in which we live, aspects of which we are cognizant and indeed proud?

Community sounds are a kind of aural portal or window into the complexity and diversity around us. In an age when so many things seem to be known or knowable, there are many sounds that convey a mystery and wildness that we lack in other dimensions of life. There are many significant and underappreciated natural sounds around us that are essential to our connection to nature and other forms of life, that are profoundly meaningful, and that are inherently therapeutic. I have come to relish the summer evening sounds of crickets, katydids, tree frogs, and night birds that lull me to sleep, and the melodic sounds of cicadas during the day that propel me forward with optimism.

The biophilic sounds in the city change over the course of the year and also help urbanites mark the seasons. A ubiquitous and beautiful sound along the east coast of the United States is the northern spring peeper (*Pseudacris crucifer*), a tiny tree frog that marks the spring and heralds the soon-to-be summer. Hearing a chorus of these frogs on a spring evening (only males sing, seeking to impress and attract mates) inserts an audible element of mystery and wildness to urban and suburban life—and the more we are accustomed to hearing their spring sounds (and the more we look forward to their arrival), the more they are a part of our urban community.

Greater knowledge of the peeper's biology in turn deepens the sense of fascination and wonder and respect. Peeper frogs, for instance, make their songs by inflating and deflating their "vocal sacs" right below their chins (when singing together, they are sometimes said to sound like jingling sleigh bells). We rarely see them singing, but we can imagine the movement when we hear the sounds. Equally fascinating, peepers produce glucose that acts as a sort of natural antifreeze, allowing them to enter a frozen state and thus protect their bodies during winter. It may be that such clever biological tricks can provide useful insights in designing for human space travel or life in similarly harsh environments on Earth, but the knowledge alone deepens appreciation of the mystery and magic of their songs. I imagine them in this frozen condition in January and February, waiting for the warm weather to melt their bodies and to release the torrent of natural sounds they make.[49]

Bird songs and calls are for many of us living in cities joyous and therapeutic and, like the frog sounds, help to fix our place in the season. I look forward to the arrival of robins in the spring and the orchestral sounds of the diverse mix of spring and summer inhabitants. Some have even observed that the winter solstice, December 21, is marked by the beginning of bird songs. Donald Kroodsma's book *Birdsongs by the Seasons* explores this in an interesting way by cataloging and recording the songs and vocalizations of birds over the months of the year. He uses sonograms and careful observation to understand the subtle nuances heard. His book provides advice about doing our own recordings of birds, but perhaps most important, it helps us to hear and understand in new ways the sounds around us. Perhaps more than anything, we urbanites must learn (again?) to become good and careful listeners of the many natural voices around us.[50]

Another popular book of bird songs, written by Peter Marler and Hans Slabbekoorn, is *Nature's Music*.[51] I'm struck by how the word *music* resonates in describing the many sounds we hear from nature, many in cities—the screech owl, the peepers, and of course the birds, among many others. Ironically, it seems that city building these days is often about major investments in the cultural infrastructure that centers around the more usual form of music we talk about—building new opera houses, concert halls, or music pavilions, rightly heralding the art and culture and uplifting and exhilarating experience of an orchestral concert or operatic aria. Yet few of us seem to appreciate the deeper primordial music that permeates the cities and suburbs in which we live and perhaps the need to invest in this natural musical infrastructure to an equal degree.

The new presence of coyotes in cities like Washington and Chicago and Los Angeles offers some promise of new auditory delight as well. While the yips and howls and barks of coyotes might elicit fear in some, for others (and most urbanites, we would hope over time) the sounds are joyous declarations of the shared biological space and the persistence of wildness in even the most apparently tamed settings.

Smell is another powerful sense that connects us to nature in many ways. It is said that humans can distinguish as many as ten thousand distinct smells. Biophilic cities are fragrant cities. The *smellscape* will vary from city to city and region to region. The scents of flowers and flowering trees, from magnolias to dogwoods, are important smells in southern cities, for instance. In northwest cities Douglas fir and ponderosa pine create scents quite distinct from their urban counterparts in the Southwest, such as mesquite. It is hard to overstate the importance of natural odors, and they are not always the most obvious ones in cities: They include the seasonal scent of fallen leaves and the distinctive scent of rain and rain showers. In cities these odors are not always pleasant (e.g., think garbage, diesel fumes), but many are pleasant, essential place-fixing elements.

The Nature Behind (and Ahead)

Every bit of nature visible in cities today, every landform or hydrologic feature, is to some degree shaped by the life history of that point on Earth. The nature of cities is heavily informed by and to a certain extent viewed through the prism of ancient life, of a deeper, longer process of evolution and change and reformulation. There are often practical management reasons for wanting to know these things (what does the ancient geology of place tell us about why building pilings and foundations fail in earthquakes, for instance?), but there are many other reasons to understand the deep history of a place. It can be argued that we will never have a clear sense of who we are as a species, never completely understand ourselves, without understanding our longer history. Biophilia is the ultimate demonstration of this, in the sense that our present psychology and emotional health are dependent on an ancient evolutionary brain. A deeper understanding of geological and ecological history help answer the question of where we live and help to define a deeper, more meaningful understanding of home. We lack that in many American communities (most, perhaps) and in turn lack the rudder and stability and perspective that a longer history can provide us. This deeper knowledge can strengthen commitment and caring for the places in which we live. And it is just fun and enjoyable to spend time learning things about places that go beyond the superficial, beyond the surface.

In San Francisco much can be learned about current nature in the city by understanding the historic environment. Few residents appreciate that nearly half of the San Francisco peninsula, the northern and western portions, is comprised of ancient sand dunes. It's an exotic and deeply interesting geologic context, and much of the city's development past has been about battling those dunes. Formed of material eroded from the Sierra Nevada mountain range, it has given rise to unique floral species, for instance, plants with deep roots and small flowers, an adaptation more common to desert circumstances. San Francisco has been described in the geology literature as comprised largely of high hills of bedrock poking through a blanket of sand dunes, with important areas of mudflats and tidal marshes (many of which have been filled to make room for development). These contemporary land and community alterations are important, of course, for understanding the extent of ecological loss or damage as well as the vulnerability of current residents and buildings to such dangers as earth liquefaction. These longer-term forces and circumstances have shaped and molded over millennia the nature that we see today and provide us with unusual perspective on where we have come and where we are going.

On a visit to Iowa City, Iowa, I had the chance to visit a very unusual park centered around the city's deeper geologic history. In the aftermath of the severe floods that occurred up and down the Mississippi watershed in 1993, a quarter-mile stretch of bedrock from the Devonian period of the Paleozoic (410–360 million years ago) was opened up near Iowa City for all to see. Later named the Devonian Fossil Gorge, it has become a popular state park and a local attraction of some pride to residents.

Any visitor spending any amount of time in Iowa City today will likely be taken to the gorge to see the visible fossils of an amazing assortment of critters and creatures. They include corals, crinoids ("a kind of ancient sea urchin with a somewhat cup-shaped body and five or more feathery arms"), and brachiopods ("marine invertebrates with a pair of arms bearing tentacles inside bivalve shells").[52] It's a tactile experience that allows kids to touch the fossils and trace them with their fingers. They can take paper, as many do when visiting, and trace the critters, and then dart and jump among the boulders and rocks and splash in the environment in which the fossils are found. It's a prized destination for local kids, and it's not hard to see why.

Kids seem especially intrigued by the idea that these Iowa waters were populated by rather large fish. Most notable is the *arthrodire*, a rather fierce-looking armored predator with a complex-looking hinged jaw, and probably eight to ten feet in length. Fossils from one of these fish were found at the site and have since been moved to a Corps of Engineers museum not far away. There is something especially vivid and striking about imagining such large fish in places now occupied by shopping centers and cornfields.

The park offers the community a common understanding of the fascinating geological and biological history of the city. Tom Dean, who teaches at the University of Iowa, speaks of the role of the gorge in helping residents to "sink taproots of connection into place with those closest to us through regular family visits."[53] It provides residents with a long-term fix on their origins and a very vivid reminder that their current position in time is but a tiny placeholder in the larger story of Earth. And another thing it may do is evoke in us a humbleness and thinking beyond ourselves, a kind of antidote to the hubris and self-centeredness that often characterize our view of environment, perhaps especially so in cities.

There is a very long tower inside the National Museum of Natural History, in Washington, D.C., that visually presents the history of Earth: The time of humans is a minute sliver at the very top, and that is a very useful image to keep in mind. As a species, humans have been cultivating the earth and growing crops, for about 10,000 years, yet leaf-cutter ants have been cultivating and gardening fungi for some 40 million years.

The longer arcs of history and geology are great ways to frame present-day cities. Leslie Day, in her *Field Guide to the Natural World of New York City*,[54] frames the discussion of the abundant nature in New York in terms of its fascinating geological and natural history. The story for her begins 400 million years ago, when the site of modern-day New York was then "towering mountain peaks," the gradual erosion of which has left behind many of the landscape features visible today. Glaciation and the advance and retreat of ice sheets are much of the story. At the end of the last ice age, the flora and fauna we know today began to emerge:

> As the climate warmed, new plants took root in New York, replacing the arctic willows and grasses. Conifers such as spruce, pine, and fir trees dominated the area until seven thousand years ago, when hemlocks and broadleaf deciduous trees such as oaks and chestnuts created mixed forests. Humans first arrived in the area about this time and, with the warming climate, the Ice Age mammals disappeared. Five thousand years ago, about the same time that human villages became more common, hickories replaced hemlocks, and holly and birch grew in the oak and chestnut forests.[55]

Who knew that Manhattan was such a biologically rich place when Henry Hudson arrived on September 12, 1609? Thanks to the work of landscape ecologist Eric Sanderson, of the Wildlife Conservation Society at the Bronx Zoo, we now have a much better idea of what Manhattan was like at that time. Through painstaking research, a combination of analyzing historical maps, soil profiles, hydrologic and topographic conditions, and even the settlement patterns and history of the native Lenape people who inhabited the island, Sanderson has constructed an intricate and enlightening natural history of this now densely developed city.[56] The result is, among other things, a new appreciation for the biological and ecological diversity of the island. Boasting fifty-five different ecological communities ("more than is found on the average coral reef or in most rainforests of similar size"[57]) and a unique ecological setting (e.g., positioned on an estuary at the southern extent glaciation), *Mannahatta*—the Lenape word for the island, meaning "Island of Many Hills"—was a wealthy place indeed.

Sanderson and his colleagues, through the creative use of GIS and digital imaging, have managed to generate a fascinating set of renderings depicting what Manhattan might have looked like in 1609, as contrasted with modern views from the same vantages. The result is a very successful effort at, as Sanderson says, "draping" this urban landscape "with a forgotten ecology."[58] This is a useful exercise by which to stoke the imagination and stimulate thinking about future nature in this city. And indeed that is what he does in the last chapter of his study, imagining what Manhattan and greater New York might look like four hundred years into the future. "Infused with the spirit of Mannahatta," the future city is one where much food is grown locally, where energy is produced from local renewable sources (e.g., capturing tidal energy), where buildings capture solar energy and breath (not unlike wigwams or longhouses), where the urban environment is abundant with green rooftops and rain gardens and permeable paving, and where residents reconnect with their extensive waterfront. And future urbanization patterns, influenced by commitments to sustainability and the dynamics of climate change, will result in dense settlements with farms and forests and natural habitats in between.[59] Taken together, the vision is not unlike the future sketched in the pages to follow.

Concluding Thoughts

The *wildness* of cities, the *nature* of cities, extends well beyond the usual areas we tend to think of. It is not just the established public parks or green areas in a city but much more: the trees on streets, courtyards, rooftops, creeks, and hydrological features, many of which have been hidden and highly altered. We can see signs of this remnant nature everywhere we look.

Thinking about the presence of nature in most spaces and dimensions that permeate a typical city offers a fuller view of urban biodiversity and wildness: fish and aquatic species living and traveling in the rivers and streams that move through a city; microorganisms living in the clouds; birds and bats in flight at various altitudes; ants, invertebrates, and fungi underfoot; innumerable micro-wildernesses inhabiting the spaces and crevices and soil on every corner. The city is a wild place indeed, teeming with life and wondrous for the resilience and adaptability of this life. This is, at least for most Americans, a different way of seeing and understanding cities and urban life. The everyday nature, to borrow Stephen Kellert's language, is all around us and is precious indeed.

Three

Biophilic Cities: What Are They?

While we are already designing biophilic buildings and the immediate spaces around them, we must increasingly imagine biophilic cities and should support a new kind of biophilic urbanism. Exactly what is a biophilic city, what are its key features and qualities? Perhaps the simplest answer is that it is a city that puts nature first in its design, planning, and management; it recognizes the essential need for daily human contact with nature as well as the many environmental and economic values provided by nature and natural systems.

A biophilic city is at its heart a biodiverse city, a city full of nature, a place where in the normal course of work and play and life residents feel, see, and experience rich nature—plants, trees, animals. The nature is both large and small—from treetop lichens, invertebrates, and even microorganisms to larger natural features and ecosystems that define a city and give it its character and feel. Biophilic cities cherish what already exists (and there is much, as we have already seen) but also work hard to restore and repair what has been lost or degraded and to integrate new forms of nature into the design of every new structure or built project. We need contact with nature, and that nature can also take the form of shapes and images integrated into building designs, as we will see.

I have written much in the past about green cities and green urbanism, and I continue to argue for the importance of this broader agenda. Biophilic urban design and biophilic urban planning represent one particular, albeit critical, element of green urbanism—the connection with and designing-in of nature in cities. In recognizing the innate need for a connection to nature, biophilic cities tie the argument for green cities and green urbanism more directly to human well-being than to energy or environmental conservation.

For some the vision of green cities is not especially green—placing the emphasis on such things as investments in transit, renewable energy production, and energy-efficient building systems. Again, these are all important topics as we reimagine and redefine sustainable urban living in the twenty-first century. But biophilic cities place the focus squarely on the nature, on the presence and celebration of the actual green features, life-forms, and processes with which we as a species have so intimately coevolved.

While there is much overlap between biophilic cities and green urbanism, mostly complementary, there may also be ways in which these areas diverge or part. A biophilic city, as I will elucidate below, is even more than simply a biodiverse city: It is a place that learns from nature and emulates natural systems, incorporates natural forms and images into its buildings and cityscapes, and designs and plans with nature. Celebrating an urban building that assumes the shape of a form in nature, or encouraging ornamentation and textures that build connections to place and geology and natural history, are clearly biophilic but likely outside the usual rubric of green cities. The love of and care for nature, the core value in biophilic cities, extends even beyond its borders to take steps and programs and actions that help to defend and steward over nature in other parts of the globe. And the green elements of cities serve many other important functions—they retain stormwater, sequester carbon, cool the urban environment, and moderate the impacts of air pollution, for example. For me, biophilic urbanism represents a creative mix of green urban design with a commitment to outdoor life and the protection and restoration of green infrastructure from Æthe bioregional to the neighborhood level. The ability to reach on foot, by bicycle, or by transit a park or point of wild nature is essential. Parks are a part of the story, but we need to expand our notion of how a park is used. Some cities, like New York, now encourage family camping in parks, and in many cities parks have become extended classrooms for schools. How much of a city's budget goes to actively restoring and repairing nature and to educating, celebrating, and actively working to bridge the nature disconnect? These are a few of the potential metrics.

In some cases we have good examples of cities that have established useful biophilic targets and are working toward them. New York has established the goal of providing a park or greenspace within a ten-minute walk of every resident. The city of Singapore has devoted approximately half of its ground area to nature and greenspace, an impressive achievement in what is a very dense city.

What follows below is a list of some of the qualities that are found in a biophilic city. There is no single or definitive definition, no universal meaning, for what biophilic design and planning currently encompass or for what a biophilic city looks like and is. This chapter, and the criteria and targets presented in box 3.1, are an initial attempt to flesh out some of the dimensions and some of the measures by which we might judge the biophilic bona fides of a city. The sections that follow are grouped according to

Box 3.1
Indicators of a Biophilic City

Biophilic Conditions and Infrastructure

Percentage of population within 100 meters of a park or greenspace

> *Example:* PlaNYC's target of a park or greenspace for all residents within a 10-minute walk by 2030. Evidence suggests that parks and greenspaces within 100 meters are more commonly visited; perhaps a sensible target is to provide at least one park or greenspace within 100 meters for all residents.

Existence of a connected, integrated ecological network; green urbanism from rooftop to region

> *Example:* Helsinki, Finland's regional, connected greenspace network; Keskupuesto Park provides an unbroken green wedge from old-growth forest at edge of town to very center of the city.

Percentage of city land area in wild or semi-wild nature

> *Example:* Cities must provide more than formal parks, grass median strips, and exotic landscaping; there must be areas where residents can see and experience native wild or semi-wild nature—forests, wetlands, meadows, and native vegetation. In the city of Perth, Australia, the two largest parks—Bold Park and King's Park—are largely left in native bushland. Nagoya, Japan has set aside 10 percent of its land for nature preserves. A target of 10 percent seems a reasonable and minimal target and goal.

Percentage forest cover in the city (in some regions this will be less appropriate)

> *Example:* American Forests recommends a target of 40 percent forest canopy cover over an entire metropolitan area; higher in outer areas, lower in city center locations. São Paulo, Brazil, which struggles to protect Atlantic forests, has approximately 20 percent of its jurisdiction in dense forest.

Extent and number of green urban features (e.g., green rooftops, green walls, trees)

> *Example:* One green rooftop or other urban green feature per 1,000 inhabitants, or minimum one per urban block. Chicago, for example, now has more than 500 green rooftops.

Miles per capita of walking trails

> *Example:* Anchorage, Alaska has a whopping 250 miles of trails, and with a population of about 280,000, that converts to about 1 mile of trail per 1,000 population, a relatively high level; these trails are multiseasonal and offer considerable wildness within the city's borders.

Number of community gardens and garden plots (absolute and per capita); access to community garden area

> *Example:* Seattle's P-Patch community program has established the goal of at least one community garden per 2,500 city residents.

Biophilic Activities

Percentage of population that is active in nature or outdoor clubs or organizations; number of such organizations active in the city

> *Example:* Many urban residents are active members in nature clubs, bird-watching or gardening clubs, and other organizations that encourage connections with nature and outdoor activities. One potential and reasonable target would be for at least one-quarter of a city's population to be active members and involved in one or more of such organizations.

Percentage of population engaged in nature restoration and volunteer efforts (e.g., such as Urban Bushcare), as well as absolute number

> *Example:* Brisbane, Australia has 124 active bushcare groups (known as Habitat Brisbane) and some 2,500 active volunteers; out of a city population of approximately 1 million, this represents only a .0025 participation rate. A minimum target might be to see 1–5 percent of a city's population actively participating in bushcare efforts.

Percentage of time residents spend outside (may vary depending on climate)

> *Example:* Currently most Americans spend only about 5 percent of the day outdoors. An initial target of 15–20 percent would seem reasonable, and even ambitious, depending on the climate and time of year.

Percentage of residents who actively garden (including balcony, rooftop, and community gardens)

> *Example:* Recent surveys indicate that an impressive 44 percent of the residents of Vancouver, British Columbia grow at least some of their own food.

Extent of recess and outdoor playtime in schools

> *Example:* Finland's school system provides outdoor play opportunity between each teaching segment during the school day (essentially every 45 minutes).

Biophilic Attitudes and Knowledge

Percentage of population that can recognize common species of native flora and fauna

> *Example:* At least one-third of a city's residents should be able to correctly identify a common native bird species, say, a cardinal in Richmond, Virginia.

Extent to which residents are curious about the natural world around them (as measured by a proxy such as a survey question or community experiment).

> *Example:* Residents of a city should spend, on average, a minimum of thirty minutes a day watching, exploring, or learning about the nature around them. A number of local and state governments have administered nature or wildlife awareness surveys that collect information about the amount of time spent looking at or experiencing nature, as well as the extent of knowledge about local species of flora and fauna. For instance, the Florida Backyard Wildlife Habitat Program, administered by the Florida Wildlife Extension Service, asks questions such as the following as part of its application form: "Can you comfortably identify some adult Florida butterflies?

(Yes/No) If yes, about how many species?" and "On average, how many minutes per week do you spend watching butterflies, other insects, and spiders in your yard?" (See duval.ifas.ufl.edu/pdf/lawn_and_garden/Wild_Life_Habitat_Application.pdf). Academic studies and university researchers have also collected similar information about knowledge of local nature that might also provide useful models. For instance, in an especially interesting study of bird knowledge in Wellington, New Zealand, Parker (2009) asked households to identify six local bird species (through photographs presented in a questionnaire); see also Archer and Beale (2004).

Biophilic Institutions and Governance

Adoption of a local biodiversity action plan or strategy
> *Example:* Many cities around the world have prepared biodiversity action plans, for instance, Dublin, Ireland and Capetown, South Africa.

Extent of local biophilic support organizations, for example, existence of an active natural history museum or botanical garden
> *Example:* U.S. cities such as Cleveland, Ohio have both an active local botanical garden and a natural history museum. A reasonable target is to ensure that cities have municipal organizations and capabilities equivalent to these two forms of biophilic engagement and education.

Priority given to environmental education
> *Example:* Many urban schools have outdoor classrooms and educational efforts that tie learning in traditional areas (science and math) to hands-on activities that involve learning about nature. One reasonable target is that at least half of a city's public schools operate such initiatives.

Percent of local budget devoted to nature conservation, recreation, education, and related activities
> *Example:* While there are few comparative studies, a reasonable target is that a minimum of 5 percent of a city's budget should be devoted to nature conservation, education, and restoration.

Adoption of green building and planning codes, grant programs, density bonuses, greenspace initiatives, and dark-sky lighting standards
> *Example:* Many American cities, such as Seattle and Portland, have municipal code provisions that either mandate or encourage green features and biophilic design. A city's planning code should include a combination of incentives (e.g., density bonuses) and requirements (e.g., greenspace factor) to encourage green urban features.

Number of city-supported biophilic pilot projects and initiatives
> *Example:* Many cities, such as Chicago, have seen great value in piloting new green design ideas and concepts and providing technical and financial support. A city should have under way at least five biophilic pilot projects or initiatives.

the organization of this box and suggest that biophilic cities can be described or recognized through a combination of their physical conditions and infrastructure, the undertakings and activities of their residents, their knowledge and awareness, and by the governance priorities, capacities, and commitments of their agencies and officials.

Biophilic Conditions and Infrastructure

One key way to begin to describe what a biophilic city is (or could be) is to identify some of the various conditions or circumstances that exist or to which a city aspires. How much nature is there, and is it easily reached and enjoyed? To what extent has the city invested in the essential infrastructure to permit an urban life lived in close daily contact with the natural world?

Biophilic Cities Are Places of Easily Accessible and Abundant Nature

A biophilic city is at once concerned about the ecological integrity of its network of nature and its accessibility and the ability of a resident to move from a neighborhood to larger green realms. We know from chapter 2 that cities already harbor much biodiversity, often much more than we realize and that this everyday nature imparts (or has the potential to impart) a sense of wildness and essential ecological values to urbanites.

And any conception of a biophilic city is one in which access to nature is viewed as essential to a meaningful and happy life and thus something that all individuals and neighborhoods are entitled to. Biophilic cities seek to make nature equally accessible and equally enjoyable to all residents.

The best way to access nature—parks and greenspaces, rivers and mountains, trees and forests, green rooftops—in a city while protecting it is open to debate. Some of the green qualities will be beyond the control of a city—the underlying diversity of species and habitat (e.g., consider the biologically rich cities in the tropics, or in environments such as southern California or South Africa with Mediterranean climates high in species endemism) or topography. Others will be a function more of historical happenstance (why a particular feature or habitat was not developed or altered), but many will be within the intentional grasp of the city and a function of their commitments and efforts.

The physical network of greenspaces and nature at the city and metropolitan level—its larger patterns of green infrastructure—is of course essential and a clear manifestation of green commitments and priorities over time. Increasingly we recognize the need to integrate and tie together the many individual green features and neighborhood parks that exist in a city into a more holistic ecological network. A number of cities have done this quite successfully. Helsinki, Finland, for instance, has one of the most impressive urban green networks, integrating larger natural features (Keskupuisto Central Park that runs in an unbroken wedge from old-growth forest on the edge of the city right to the center of the city) with smaller features at the neighborhood and street level.

Many cities have developed regional greenspace plans and visions. American cities include Boulder, Colorado (its greenbelt now consists of over 30,000 acres of protected land), Portland, Oregon, and Chicago (e.g., Chicago Wilderness). Impressive European city efforts include Hannover, Germany's 87-killometer-long Green Ring, and Vitoria-Gasteiz, Spain's Green Belt. The latter shows the great value of joining dense and compact urban form with land conservation. In Vitoria-Gasteiz, urban neighborhoods are but a short walk away from large natural areas, including Salburua Park, a former airport converted into an important wetland for migratory birds. Extensive trails and a city nature center are part of the biophilic infrastructure of this city. The city has placed much importance on the Green Belt and on integrating nature into the life of this city, and it is now working on a second or outer Green Belt, building on the provincial conservation plan, that will allow residents to reach even more distant natural points and connect with the ancient sheepherding past of the region.

We know from research that there are many biophilic benefits derived from views of nature—forests or mountains from the window of a building or from street level, for example. As discussed in chapter 1, views of nature have been found to have significant therapeutic and cognitive benefits and of course are an essential element in unique sense of place. Some cities, such as Denver, have been blessed with spectacular mountain views (in this case, the Rockies) and have taken steps to protect those views for visitors to municipal parks. Cities like Vancouver, British Columbia or Cape Town, South Africa are blessed with topography and natural environments that are visually prominent and striking. Vancouver has emphasized a strategy of accommodating population growth through slender high-rise towers yet has placed great importance on siting and spacing those buildings to ensure views of the city's spectacular surroundings.

A gauge or measure of this naturalness might be achieved through some proxy measures in common use, such as overall tree canopy cover or imperviousness, but there is probably no single measure that captures all of the pieces of a green and natural city.

Biophilic Cities Are Rich, Textured, Multisensory Environments

A biophilic city is one that is full of varied sights, sounds, smells, and textures, many but not all of which are natural. It is a city of rich and deep sensory experiences. The sources of these biophilic sensory experiences are many, from the textures, shapes, and colors of buildings, to the trees and flora and other green elements in urban environments, to the many sounds of life all around.

Sound, especially the sound associated with nature, is an especially undervalued dimension in urban planning and design today, and the biophilic city seeks to counterbalance the usual ocular or visual bias by emphasizing the importance of sounds and hearing in the city. The biophilic city nurtures and cultivates these sounds, as modes of connection with the natural world and as therapeutic and pleasurable aspects of urban living. From the squawking caw-caw of crows and the daytime rhythmic songs of cicadas, to the nighttime lulls of tree frogs, crickets, katydids, and screech owls, the auditory dimensions of urban life are absolutely essential in a biophilic city.

Of course the noise produced in cities, as opposed to the natural sounds, is also important but in a more negative context. There is evidence that automobile noise, for instance, is one factor that tends to inhibit walking to work and other outdoor activity.[1] When we manage to reduce these human and often largely auto-sourced noises, we may create the conditions in which more urbanites want to be outside and more opportunities to hear and enjoy the background natural sounds that biophilia suggests we need and want.

Many of the European cities profiled in this book emphasize natural textures and building materials and pedestrian qualities that make them profoundly biophilic. Freiburg, Germany's treatment of water—it has restored and extended its "Bächle," or little streams that bring water into the city, and these water channels run through the city's streets—is the city's most prominent element. But it is also the beautiful and textured stones that make up the squares and pedestrian spaces, the distinctive colored tiles that mark the entrances to shops, the textured building façades, even the gargoyles on the surfaces of the main church, that make viewing Freiburg from outdoors infinitely enjoyable. There is an organic nature to many of these cities that sends the message that these are places embedded in landscapes and antiquity, places that stimulate the senses and are beautiful to see, hear, and touch. These are biophilic cities of the senses.

European cities have a long-term commitment to reusing and recycling their environments and seem to deeply appreciate and care for and about them. This quality is missing in many American cities. As Yale's Stephen Kellert says, perhaps there is a connection, and it is the biophilic qualities that instill a reverence and commitment to their long-term durability: "In some of our European cities one of the reasons I think they're far more sustainable is not because they're using energy efficient systems necessarily, although we like them to, but because they take such investment in those places that they recycle them generation after generation. . . . If you start to look at those places what makes people develop that sense of attachment, responsibility and stewardship for those places . . . they're replete with biophilic elements, in their scale, in their materials, in the shapes and forms that mimic and simulate natural patterns. . . . They're rich biophilic environments."[2]

Biophilic Cities Are Inspired by and Mimic Nature

Janine Benyus's groundbreaking book *Biomimicry*[3] has been instrumental in changing the way we think about design, as has been the inspiring design work of architect Bill McDonough.[4] Benyus's key message is that nature has many lessons to convey, that thousands of years of evolution have allowed plants and animals to do things and accomplish feats that we might and should seek to replicate and mimic in design. As she notes, "I believe it is part of our nature to be drawn to life's mastery and to try, with equal parts awe and envy, to do what birds and fish and insects can do."[5] Benyus and other advocates of the practical value of biomimicry argue that it makes little sense to ignore the 3.8 billion years of research and development that other species supply.

Biophilic cities reflect a humility that understands the wisdom of nature and natural systems and the need to learn from them and model design and planning after them. McDonough is famous for imploring us to design "buildings like trees, cities like forests." A city the functions like a tree is a model for our time, as we imagine cities that are carbon neutral and energy-balanced (that produce as much power as they need and live within the limits of current solar income), that are zero-waste, and that integrate and celebrate diversity (from which cities will become more resilient in the face of climate change and a highly dynamic world). While not perfect examples, McDonough and his colleagues have managed to build structures that do function nearly as trees do—the environmental studies building at Oberlin College, for instance, that produces more energy than it needs, that collects and treats all of its stormwater on site, that treats its wastewater through a solar-aquatic *living machine* (treating and breaking down waste through a system of plants, aquatic species, and microorganisms, in compact vertical tanks). The bigger challenge is to scale up the organic model to operate at the level of a city and region, and it is this challenge that links the sustainability enterprise most closely to planning.

The growing importance of biomimicry in design and policy and engineering is undeniable, and it is an exciting prospect to imagine how future cities and urban environments might be reshaped in ways that are informed and inspired by nature. Buildings and urban built environments have already exhibited biomimical insights. Green building design is perhaps the place where biomimicry is most evident, but there is increasing potential to apply the natural principles and design standards found and tested in nature to cities. Box 3.2 presents Benyus's ten design strategies from nature, and each finds obvious and significant application to cities and built environments.

One of the early examples of a building based on biomimicry is found in Harare, Zimbabwe—the office complex called Eastgate Centre. Designed by Zimbabwean architect Michael Pearce, the complex is inspired by the design of termite colonies, specifically the techniques they use to maintain a constant temperature and humidity. Like a termite mound, Eastgate draws its air in from the base of the building, cools the air by sending it underground, and then circulates this air up and through the structure.

There are many green building examples as well as other elements of sustainable urban design and living that find inspiration and guidance

---

Box 3.2
Biomimicry Strategies for Cities

1. Use waste as a resource.
2. Diversify and cooperate to fully use the habitat.
3. Gather and use energy efficiently.
4. Optimize rather than maximize.
5. Use materials sparingly.
6. Don't foul their nests.
7. Don't draw down resources.
8. Remain in balance with the biosphere.
9. Run on information.
10. Shop locally.

Source: Benyus, 2002.

from nature. High-speed urban rail and intercity rail is one example. Notable is the design of the Japanese Shinkansen bullet train: Its nose is based on that of a kingfisher.[6] Geckos, lizards that walk easily along vertical surfaces, even upside down, are being studied for what they can tell us about waterless adhesion. The reptile's secret is a dense network of nano-sized hairs on its feet. Researchers are now converting this knowledge into a host of applications, many of which may directly apply in the management of future cities—for instance, new forms of adhesion that allow robotic cleaning and maintenance of windows and high-rise building spaces. A team of engineers at UC–Berkeley has been focused on designing new tires, perhaps for use on fleets of urban buses, that take advantage of the amazing gripping qualities of the gecko's feet.[7]

At Michigan State University, researchers have been developing the prototype of a robotic fish, mimicking the natural swimming patterns and abilities of living fish. Entire schools of such robotic fish may be set off in urban streams and rivers to provide highly useful real-time monitoring data about water quality, hydrology, and climate. According to MSU professor Elena Litchman, "With these patrolling fish we will be able to obtain information at an unprecedentedly high spatial and temporal resolution. Such data are essential for researchers to have a more complete picture of what is happening under the surface as climate change and other outside forces disrupt the freshwater ecosystems. It will bring environmental monitoring to a whole new level."[8]

There are many other examples and possibilities: producing energy in cities through photovoltaics with improved efficiency designed with tree and plant leaves as a model; improvements in the efficiency of wind turbine blades, by learning from flippers of humpback whales (which contain bumps that significantly improve efficiency); learning how to extract potable drinking water from humid air, learning from insects that do this with great efficiency.

A number of paint products now on the market seek to simulate the pollution-cleansing power of trees and nature. The company Ecopurer, for instance, now markets a series of paint products for various surfaces in cities—roadway surfaces, tunnels, buildings—that through catalytic chemical reactions (using titanium dioxide) help to transform urban air pollutants into more benign substances. The company's Web page describes how the product works in terms of mimicking nature: "A photocatalytic reaction imitates the chlorophylic photosynthesis of trees in their absorption and transformation of pollutants into non-toxic elements, using just light and air."[9]

Much of the new importance given to cities is a recognition, a re-framing really, of the ultimate source of environmental and resource consumption, as well as a recognition of where the real potential for a more sustainable future lies. The concept of the ecological footprint, developed by William Rees and Mathis Wackernagel, fosters in turn a view of a city as an organic entity, analogous to the human body, requiring inputs and generating outputs.[10] We now begin to connect the loss of tropical rain forests, the emissions of carbon, and the consumption of oil to feed ourselves, produce and heat our homes, sequester the carbon associated with our lifestyles, and so on. The ecological footprint concept and method (what Rees originally called ecological footprint analysis[11]) profoundly shifted our collective understanding of cities: They depend on an extensive hinterland, extracting and appropriating the carrying capacities of faraway regions and countries. And, at least for northern industrial cities, size of this footprint is very large and growing. A recent study of London's ecological footprint found, for example, that the land area needed to support this city of 8 million was nearly 300 times the physical size of the city itself. The number also offers hope and guidance for change—in the case of London, much of the footprint is associated with importation of food from long distances, providing incentives for advocates supporting initiatives to support more local and regional food production.

The last several decades have seen a rise in explicit efforts to apply organic or natural models of how nature works to the design of buildings and cities. Cities are in many ways indeed analogous to living organisms—they require material inputs for survival, produce waste, and have a complex and interconnected metabolism. Yet our city planning and urban management policies often fail to acknowledge this complex metabolism. We treat the inputs and outputs and resources discretely and individually, not holistically. Our move toward sustainable cities will require an important shift in thinking of cities not as linear resource-extracting machines but as complex metabolic systems with flows and cycles where, ideally, the things that have traditionally been viewed as negative outputs (e.g., solid waste, wastewater) are reenvisioned as productive inputs to satisfy other urban needs, including food, energy, and clean water. A sustainable urban metabolism has several goals at once: to reduce the extent of the material and resource flows required, to convert linear flows to circular flows (closed loops), and to source and derive the inputs in the most equitable and least ecologically destructive way possible.

Many advocates of green cities and green urbanism describe a sustainable city as a closed-loop city, one that, like nature, wastes nothing and operates with a circular metabolism.[12] Only a few working examples of

Figure 3.1 Masdar City.

such cities exist. In *Green Urbanism* I describe the efforts of the city of Stockholm, and the flagship green neighborhood Hammarby Sjöstad, which has been designed from the beginning to take advantage of resource flows and to begin to connect inputs and outputs. As in nature, nothing is wasted. For example, at Hammarby hundreds of flats are equipped with natural gas stoves that burn biogas extracted from organic household waste from the neighborhood!

More recent sustainable city designs are also being created with this closed-loop philosophy and with the principles of natural systems in mind. These include Dongtan eco-city in China (now on hold) and Masdar City, the carbon-neutral new town near Abu Dhabi, in the United Arab Emirates. In the case of Dongtan, emphasis has been placed on producing all of the energy needed for the new town from renewable energy sources, as well as the food needed for residents from fields and rooftops nearby. The city will function in a closed-loop fashion, with agricultural wastes (e.g., rice husks) used to produce power, for instance.

Masdar City is being designed to take full advantage of the natural climate and conditions of its desert setting. This includes orienting buildings to minimize the amount of direct sunlight hitting buildings' sides and windows, and building in masses and heights to shade narrow streets while also allowing natural flows of breezes. It too plans to produce much or all of its own energy locally and aspires to being a carbon-neutral city. The center of Masdar has been designed (LAVA Architects) with sunflower-like structures, "solar sun shades" that "open up during the day . . . to protect the courtyard from the blazing sun, and at night the shades collapse to release heat out into the air."[13] The architects have called these shades the "Petals from Heaven," which along with the other features of the plaza will draw residents to this "Oasis of Life":

> The ability to control ambient temperature at all times of the day is the key to making the Plaza a compulsive destination. The gorges pull inhabitants into the loop. The "Petals from Heaven" open and close; protect pedestrians from the sun; capture, store, and release heat; adjust the angle of shade based on the position of the sun. The heat sensitive lamps adjust the level of lighting to the proximity of pedestrians. The water features ebb and flow based on the intensity of ground temperatures.[14]

LAVA's description of this plaza as a "living, breathing, adaptive environment" is a fitting characterization of a city that will include so many biophilic features.

Biophilic Cities Exhibit and Celebrate the Shapes and Forms of Nature

Many advocates of biophilic design define it, in part, by the many visual connections and references made to the natural world—the symbols, pictures, shapes, and natural designs—that make their way into our cities and neighborhoods. They appear on building façades, on street signs (and street names), or on sidewalks and pedestrian spaces and can even be seen in the shapes and forms taken by the buildings and architecture in cities.

An important dimension of a biophilic city, these natural shapes and forms are beautiful, reassuring, and valuable touch points of our deep evolutionary bonds with nature. Though not often the subject of analysis or tallying-up, their presence in cities is another measure of our biophilic sensibilities.

Urban building designs are obvious and important places where biophilic forms and shapes find expression. A number of architects and urbanists in the last several decades have taken great inspiration from nature and have reimagined the cities as growing organic entities. These organic urbanists include Ton Alberts, Paolo Soleri, Luc Schuiten, Vincent Callebaut, and Richard Register. And more historically the design work of Antoni Gaudí, and more recently Fredriesch Hundertwasser, are highly organic and referential of nature.

Ton Alberts was a strong proponent of organic architecture and designed delightful buildings with shapes and forms drawn from nature. A

Dutch architect, Alberts was best known for the ING bank headquarters building in the Bijlmer district in Amsterdam. Designed around a series of light wells, the structure brings a great deal of natural light, vegetation, and water into the interior spaces, but the exterior also invokes nature in a very pleasing way. Often referred to as a "ground-hugger" (as contrasted with a skyscraper), the structure did indeed seem to grow from the ground like a plant or tree.

In more recent years there have been a variety of plans, some fanciful and grandiose, to build new cities that take the shape and form of a natural system or a specific natural element. Belgian architect Luc Schuiten has put forth the idea of the "vegetal city" and offers some beautiful visual renderings of what buildings and urban districts might look like, with shapes and building lines that are leaflike and seemingly vine covered and defined. His recent exhibit "Vegetal City: Dreaming the Green Utopia" is an inspiring display and development of these natural design ideas.

Another Belgian designer, Vincent Callebaut, has made a splash on the international scene by proposing and rendering designs for a floating "Lilypad City." A response to rising sea levels, this city of fifty thousand would produce more power than it needs (through solar and wind and wave energy) and would grow all the food and collect all the water its residents will need.[15] It would also be a city with no cars and no roads, an "amphibious" city, in Callebaut's words.

The timeless design work of Antoni Gaudí, whose work forms much of what is architecturally distinctive about Barcelona, is also highly biophilic. His designs, which include Casa Batlló, Casa Milà, the Sagrada Família, and Parc Güell, among others, include prominent biophilic elements. Often plants and animals figure into the designs, as the nativity façade on the Sagrada Família illustrates, including turtles holding up columns. A main feature of Parc Güell is Gaudí's famous dragon, composed of a mix of multicolored tiles, stone, and ceramic. The rooftop of the Casa Batlló, along the Paseo de Gracia, reminds one of the shimmering scales of a fish, and many of his buildings include undulating, rounded walls and distinctive shapes and colors that reference and connect to nature.

More recently, the work of some notable contemporaries has been incorporating organic architectural elements and building designs inspired by nature. Spanish architect Santiago Calatrava's designs, for instance, creatively connect with their unique natural settings and often incorporate organic elements. The design of the Milwaukee Art Museum, one of his first designs in the United States and located on the city's lakefront, is a case in point. The museum expansion "incorporates multiple elements inspired by the Museum's lakefront location. Among the many maritime elements in Calatrava's design are: movable steel louvers inspired by the wings of a bird; a cabled pedestrian bridge with a soaring mast inspired by the form of a sailboat and a curving single-storey galleria reminiscent of a wave."[16]

The design for the new Chicago Spire is perhaps Calatrava's most dramatic inspiration from nature. When finished in 2011 it will be the second-highest structure in the world. It is explicitly designed after the curving form of a nautilus seashell, visually arresting and unlike any other high-rise structure. Calatrava has said, "Inspired by nature, by the interaction of earth, water and air . . . the principles I follow are based on repetition. This reminds you of nature because nature often works in patterns."[17] This residential tower will contain 150 stories, with each building floor turned 2 percent from the one below, mimicking the natural spiral chambered shell and ensuring a unique set of views from floor to floor. It will incorporate a number of green features, including the use of geothermal energy and a system for recycling rainwater. While construction of the building has been placed on hold, a function of worsening economic conditions (and despite the sale of the $40 million penthouse unit), there is still hope for this spectacular biophilic addition to the Chicago skyline.

Zaha Hadid's design for the new performing arts center in Abu Dhabi is a striking example of biophilic architecture. Visually arresting, its windows appear shaped like leaves (or dragonfly wings). She describes the overall structure of the complex in organic, natural terms: a structure that grows upwardly, "gradually developing into a growing organism that sprouts a network of successive branches." "As it winds through the site, the architecture increases in complexity, building up height and depth and achieving multiple summits in the bodies housing the performance spaces, which spring from the structure like fruits on a vine and face westward, toward the water."[18]

Yet another biophilic building fit to this region of the world is Jean Nouvel's design for the National Museum of Qatar. The museum is comprised of a series of visually striking discs, meant to resemble the "sand roses" that form just below the surface in desert environments. As Nicolai Ouroussoff, the *New York Times* architecture critic, notes, "The building's dozens of disclike forms, intersecting at odd angles and piling up unevenly atop one another, celebrate a delicate beauty in the desert landscape that is invisible to those who have not spent time there."[19] The Nouvel design is commendable both for being biophilic in its form and for how it educates and informs about environment and desert ecology and invites a deeper awareness of and connection with this unique natural setting.

Figure 3.2 Calatrava's design for the Chicago Spire. Copyright: Santiago Calatrava LLC

Such nature-inspired buildings and urban elements help connect us visually and emotionally to nature and remind urban dwellers of the intrinsic and uplifting beauty and life of nature. A biophilic city is one where much of what we design and build affirms and celebrates these timeless natural forms and patterns.

Natural forms and shapes appear in many places in cities worldwide. In the Western Australian city of Fremantle, for instance, sidewalk designs incorporate seashells and other aquatic elements. One major pedestrian corridor in that city sports a series of sidewalk mosaics that vividly portray common species of native plants. Building façades and walls offer an additional palette for biophilic images and themes. On a recent visit to Raleigh, North Carolina, I discovered large, beautiful butterflies painted on the sides of several structures, and of course murals in many cities support similar biophilic scenes.

Biophilic Activities

A biophilic city is also about what it does—the more active ways in which its biophilic sensibilities are exercised and experienced and the many ways in which its citizens connect with and enjoy nature.

Biophilic Cities Celebrate Their Unique Nature and Biodiversity

A biophilic city ought to be judged not only by the existence of nature and natural features but also in some way by its biophilic sensibilities—that is, how important is nature and how central is it to the lives and modus operandi of a city's leaders and its populace?

A bit harder to quantify, this biophilic spirit or sensibility suggests a value dimension, the sense that residents and public officials alike recognize the importance and centrality of nature to a rich and sustainable urban life. This quality could easily fit as both an activity and an approach to governance.

Every city will have its natural spectacles—some large, others more nuanced—but a biophilic city is one that pays attention, a city that sees and conveys this sense of beauty and wonder and caring. It may be the running of steelhead trout in the Niagara River, or the appearance of orcas in Prince William Sound, or the migratory return of robins along the east coast of the United States. A biophilic city celebrates this wonder and sees in these events the opportunity to connect, to strengthen bonds, to mark the cycles of life and seasonality.

This celebrating often involves the direct experience of that bio-diversity and nature, such as watching migratory birds or visiting a park or green area, or it might be a more referential form of biophilic expression.

Some cities and towns have elevated the importance and centrality of nature by adopting as their official emblem or seal a local species of animal or plant. The Australian city of Penrith, in the state of New South Wales, for instance, has adopted the eastern water dragon (*Physignathus lesueurii lesueurii*) as the official emblem of its sustainability program. It is a distinctive species, a visually striking and interesting lizard, but more importantly the emblem serves to highlight the presence of a spectacular and fascinating resident of which many citizens of Penrith are unaware. More profoundly it is a tangible expression of the value attached to and interest and concern expressed about another local form of life. Penrith City's municipal Web site offers the following explanation for the choice of the lizard:

> The Eastern Water dragon was chosen because it lives along the banks of the many creeks and tributaries of the Nepean River and it represents the environmental, social and economic health of Penrith City. . . . Their habitat and numbers along the creek banks is a good indicator of the health of the City's waterways. They are long-living, sociable creatures, which live together in communities. In Chinese mythology the Water Dragon is a symbol of well-being and prosperity, reflecting Council's commitment to sustainable economic growth.[20]

The choice of such a mascot for a local sustainability program makes great sense, of course, but contrasts sharply with the approach taken by various elementary schools, high schools, and colleges in selecting a sports mascot. This latter approach shows very little originality and usually no attempt to connect to local ecosystems or native flora and fauna.

In Biophilic Cities Citizens Are Actively Involved in Enjoying, Watching, and Participating in the Nature around Them

We live in disconnected times. Indeed, we are profoundly disconnected from the people around us and from the places and environments that nurture and sustain us. Biophilic cities aspire to change these conditions and shift priorities such that citizens recognize and care about the nature around them.

The language we use to describe things is important on many levels. It signals the ways in which we interface and interact with everything—animate and inanimate—around us, and ultimately how much we care about and will steward over them. Just as our ability to call a person by his or her name personalizes that individual and indicates a level of care and familiarity, our ability to name things in our larger community must have the same psychological effect. The naming patterns of native peoples contrast significantly with the habits of Western European settlers. Native Americans typically had names for everything, and every natural feature or species had a meaning and importance attached to that name.

Biophilic cities can help to foster this connection to and knowledge of nature in many different ways. These include providing environmental education of all sorts, teaching natural history in schools, and offering outdoor education programs for adults that include not only classes but outings and field study opportunities.

As the indicators in box 3.1 suggest, how actively residents enjoy and participate in the nature around them is an important measure of a biophilic city. *Participation* is an interesting word to use here because it implies a level of active engagement beyond just passively observing something; it suggests a keen and active interest in the subject. Residents of a biophilic city are not removed from the nature around them but are highly aware of it and present in its midst. This enjoyment and engagement can take many different forms, of course, from walking and hiking in natural areas, to bird-watching and plant and tree identification, to organized nature events and activities, from fungi forays to nature festivals. Biophilic cities help to make it easier to enjoy nature and reflect an understanding that exposure to and enjoyment of nature are key aspects of a pleasurable and meaningful life.

Two quick gauges of how biophilic a population might be are the percentage of residents who bird-watch and the percentage who regularly garden. While there is undoubtedly a more sophisticated measure of participation, these two activities would capture much of what we are after here.

There are many potential adult outlets and venues for our need to connect with nature, and most are also intensely social. Facilitating contact with nature has the great potential to help create new friendships and build social networks, in turn helping to make urbanites healthier and happier. In San Diego, the activities of a number of "friends" of the canyons groups help to conserve and protect the canyons as a neighborhood and community resource but also provide opportunities for neighbors to interact and socialize in a way and to an extent that would otherwise not occur. In the Rose Canyon, for instance, residents from different sides of the canyon have places and opportunities to converse and come together, something that would have been difficult without the pull of nearby nature.

Cities must also begin to see the value and importance of facilitating such connections with nature and perhaps offering help and support, as in the Australian Bushcare model. Here local groups of citizens and community volunteers organize around a specific urban ecosystem—a patch of greenspace, a stream, a park—and with the help of a municipal staff person ("bushcare officer," usually) spend weekends and spare hours cleaning up, repairing, and tending over these spaces. This results not only in ecological repair but also in making friends, rebuilding community, and becoming more embedded in place and environment.

Creatively involving citizens in the conducting of science is another way to intimately engage people with the nature around them. In San Diego, citizens have been trained to become "parabotanists" (like paralegals), helping to collect plant specimens in this highly biodiverse county. There are now two hundred citizens serving as parabotanists, working to collect plant data for the San Diego County Plant Atlas Project (begun in 2002). The project records plants on a 3-square-mile grid. Parabotanists are now steered to collecting on grid squares where less plant data exists. Once they sign up for a square, they are mailed maps and permits from the San Diego Natural History Museum. In this most floristically biodiverse county in the United States, recording and protecting this biodiversity hotspot takes on special importance. The Plant Atlas will eventually result in an Internet-accessible, databased plant atlas based on vouchered specimens. There are more than fifteen hundred native species of plants in San Diego County to document and record, and citizens here play an important role. The San Diego Natural History Museum provides training for the volunteers, who then collect and press the plants and record data about the plants' location. A museum botanist verifies plant identification.

Based on an earlier citizen scientist program run for San Diego County's Bird Atlas, the program not only creatively involves citizens in areas where they can be of real service to science but also has a social element—bringing people together and providing an element of fun (parties). Parabotanists also receive certain additional benefits for their work, including discounts at the museum, opportunities to attend museum events and lectures for free, and access to field trips and other events.

Biophilic Cities Actively Encourage Us to Connect with Nature

In a biophilic city it should be easy and relatively effortless to enjoy nature and the outdoors, and there should be many opportunities to participate in the biophilic life of city and region. There are ideally many different local groups and social networks that offer both contact with nature and opportunities for friendship and socializing.

A biophilic city, then, is a city with an extensive and robust social capital, to extend Robert Putnam's concept.[21] Evidence is compelling that we need extensive friendships and social contact to be healthy and happy, as well as our contact with nature, so finding creative ways to combine these needs becomes an important goal in the biophilic city. I have been calling this *natural* social capital, acknowledging that there are many ways that learning about and experiencing nature can also help to nurture friendships and help to overcome the increasing levels of social isolation felt by Americans. How many social organizations or clubs, or community events or activities, explicitly focus around the unique nature of cities? The extent of creative social possibilities is almost limitless.

These biophilic organizations and activities make contact with nature more enjoyable and attractive and help to nudge us to spend more time in natural pursuits. A broad range of organizations, some public and some private, can help in supporting the education and engagement of citizens. One measure of a biophilic city is the extent of the organizational support, the quality and reach of its biophilic organizations that can actively work to nudge us toward nature.

Bird-watching and nature hikes through the city might be one option, but there should be many: swimming, canoeing, and kayaking in urban waters, visiting parks near and far, or experiencing nature on a sidewalk or rooftop or building façade as one walks to work or to the subway, among many others.

Biophilic cities are cities that work to expand the opportunities to spend time outside and in close proximity to nature. In part, this means rethinking the ways parks and greenspaces are used. New York City has been a leader in creating opportunities for urbanites to camp on weekends in city parks. The program occurs in the summer and is quite popular. In 2009, family camping took place in every borough of the city. These camping evenings are quite enjoyable and exciting, especially from the perspective of kids. The city's Parks and Recreation Department provides the tents and sleeping bags, and there are typically barbecues, night hikes, sky watching, and even s'mores!

In many parts of the United States, family nature clubs have been formed to facilitate hikes and nature trips. One such club, Kids in the Valley Adventuring (KIVA), was formed by Virginia-based parents (Chip and Ashley Donahue) to help make it easier for families and kids to get outside.[22] KIVA organizes a series of nature events in the Roanoke area of Virginia, as well as hikes and visits to nature centers, advertised in the local paper. Similar groups are forming in other parts of the country. Nature Strollers was formed by two New York State mothers who noticed few other parents on

Figure 3.3 A neighborhood tree house with kids playing. Photo credit: Tim Beatley

their nature walks. They organize weekly walks, under the auspices of the Orange County (NY) Audubon Society. The mission is "to support parents in their role as primary interpreters of nature for their families; to provide opportunities for families to enjoy unstructured time outdoors; to familiarize families with local trails, refuges, sanctuaries and preserves; and to develop networks among families with a common interest in nature."[23] The weekly walks are usually less than a mile in distance, about an hour long, and suited to a toddler or baby stroller. Such citizen initiatives and new community organizations hold considerable promise in making it easier to get outside and in overcoming some of the inertia usually involved.

Biophilic cities work hard to entice residents to spend time outside and to connect with the nature around. Perhaps this means supporting a network of nature coaches.

Some possible models of this include the Urban Park Rangers that exist in a few cities, including New York and Los Angeles. Here a corps of uniformed rangers staff city parks and nature centers, interpreting and giving tours. In some cities and countries there has been an emphasis on training nature guides. In Sweden there is an interesting program to train and certify nature guides, who earn money giving walking tours and talks at various parks and nature sites. Supported through a combination of funding from local and county governments and the Swedish Society of Nature Conservation, it is a clever way to entice residents out for a walk on weekends and at the same time help provide work for the underemployed. The certified nature guides go through a training program on effective teaching techniques and become experts on native flora and fauna. The tours and talks charge a small amount and are very popular.

Time spent outside can also take the form of food production and growing at least a portion of one's food. In many dense cities worldwide, amazing numbers of people are directly growing food in backyard gardens, in allotment gardens, and on balconies and rooftops. One survey by the Canadian Office of Urban Agriculture found a surprisingly high percentage of residents of the Greater Vancouver area—some 44 percent—grew at least some of their own food or lived in a household with those who did.[24] There is relatively little data about this, but the extent of urbanites directly involved in tilling, sowing, watering, weeding, and harvesting food is one potential measure of the extent of biophilia.

Biophilic Cities Connect Us to Our Climate

In too many parts of our country today there is a profound disconnect from the climatic conditions and forces that shape those environments. It has become too easy perhaps to withdraw to the warmth (or cool) of our homes and office buildings, experiencing the outdoor elements primarily when we move from car to building and back again.

Does it have to be this way? Is there not a sensibility that accepts, indeed celebrates, the climate and weather conditions that exist? Could learning more about, and actively celebrating and enjoying, the weather serve to deepen our appreciation of and commitments to place?

Figure 3.4 Western Australian sunset. Photo credit: Tim Beatley

Part of this is about the attitudes we bring to the places in which we live. I'm reminded of the experience with outdoor strolling and eating in Copenhagen, Denmark. As Jan Gehl, one of the most passionate advocates of pedestrian culture, reminds us, the gradual (though dramatic) conversion of much of central Copenhagen into a pedestrian district met with considerable nay-saying. People said, "Danes are not Italians," he is fond of remembering. But of course the Strøget and pedestrian walking areas have proven them wrong, and the season of outdoor eating has been extending each year. From 1962, when the Strøget was first pedestrianized, the extent of pedestrian spaces in the city's center has grown dramatically, from 15,800 square meters to 99,770 square meters in 2005.[25]

One interesting accommodation is that many restaurants now provide their customers with blankets (along with the menu). You are encouraged to enjoy sitting and eating outside, and perhaps to extend your comfort zone.

The number of outdoor café chairs more than doubled between 1986 and 2005 (from 2,970 to 7,020), a period Gehl and Gemzoe refer to as the "golden age" for Copenhagen's outdoor cafés.[26] A cultural shift and learning have accompanied the planning and public policy. There are many reasons to encourage outdoor living and lifestyles, but at the end of the day it's about enhancing quality of life.

Copenhagen also has an extensive network of parks and green-spaces and adopted an ambitious park policy in 2003.[27] Among the city's goals is to expand the opportunities for safe swimming along its harbor and shorelines. Improvement in harbor water quality has been so great that the city has already been able to open several places in the harbor for public swimming.

Copenhagen recently released an ambitious vision for its future, as-piring to be an "eco-metropole" for the year 2015. Envisioning a "green and blue capital city," the plan states the goal that by 2015 "90% of Copen-hageners must be able to walk to a park, a beach or a sea swimming-pool in less than 15 minutes."[28] The city is already at 60 percent, impressive in a dense city, and a function of an enlightened regional plan and long-standing efforts at park planning that makes it easy to access green areas. The city's efforts to make it easier and safer to get around by bicycle also further strengthen this outdoor culture and lifestyle in Copenhagen. The vision also sets a target for more time spent outdoors and in these natural areas. By 2015, Copenhageners "will visit the city's parks, natural areas, sea swim-ming-pools and beaches twice as often as they do today."

While living in Australia, my family and I were impressed by how many families tended to cook and eat meals outside in public parks and spaces. This was made possible by cities' equipping virtually every park with a set of public gas-grills for barbecuing. These were fairly large barbecues, accommodating the cooking needs of multiple families at once and not requiring any special key or reservation—just the turn of a switch. And Australians, generally exuding a cultural friendliness, showed no hesitation at cooking alongside one or more strangers. I recall watching as several families shared, without much apparent stress, the cooking space of a public bar-becue with a man who appeared to be homeless and exhibiting some slightly odd behaviors. He was not only accommodated in the cooking flow but was included in the lively conversation as well. In Australia, being out-side is made easier by a combination of climate and culture but reinforced as well by sensible planning and design decisions.

In bigger ways, the climate should become a key design element in city planning and city building. Brisbane's Queen Street Mall is a good ex-ample: An open-air pedestrian district with extensive shading entices resi-dents to be outside by effectively moderating the impacts of sun and heat. And through its CitySmart initiative, Brisbane is seeking to dramatically ex-pand its tree canopy coverage and thus the natural shading and cooling.

Throughout Australia, moreover, there is a return to building and project designs that incorporate awnings and other low-tech shading devices and windows that permit cross-ventilation and natural cooling.

Biophilic Attitudes and Knowledge

A biophilic city can also be described and characterized by the extent of the knowledge about local nature exhibited by its residents. Biophilic attitudes and knowledge, then, are an important, if often overlooked, category, in part because so many of the other biophilic conditions and activities in one way or another rely on these attitudinal and value underpinnings.

In Biophilic Cities Citizens Are Knowledgeable about the Biodiversity and Nature around Them

In the first chapter of this book I described the current and disappointingly low level of knowledge about native species of flora and fauna and the inability of many to correctly identify common species of trees, plants, and birds. Limited ability of an urban population to recognize local nature is one potential indicator of the extent of general disconnect from the natural world. It does not bode well for future conservation either, as residents of a biophilic city can be expected to declare, in essence, "This is mine, it is a part of my community, and I will care for it and steward over it."

In addition, then, to local nature knowledge and recognition are attitudes about the importance of contact with nature, the priority given to spending time outside, the value residents see in natural contact, and the general level of care for and commitment to nature. All are indicative of a city's biophilic credentials, and while these attitudes and knowledge are certainly instrumental to other biophilic goals (getting residents outside), they are also important in their own right.

Helping a city become more biophilic will rely heavily on environmental education, and creative ways will be needed to build commitment of urban populations to nature and to foster a strong urban environmental ethic. Nurturing a biophilic ethic, to be most effective, should begin at an early age but can happen at any stage in life. This can occur in many ways, and there are many public and private initiatives that teach about nature and build these important value foundations. Continuing education and adult learning can focus on nature knowledge in older residents. Experiential and field-based programs can encourage citizens of any age to learn about and recognize nature while having fun.

School-based environmental education is also essential. One very good example of this in Denver, Colorado is SPREE, the South Platte River Environmental Education program. Aimed at kids in kindergarten to 5th grade, SPREE is a partnership between the Denver public schools and the Greenway Foundation, focused around the ecology of the South Platte River (a river that runs some ten miles through the city of Denver). In nine participating schools, the South Platte is the "centerpiece of their instruction and curriculum."[29] Children make trips to the river, participate in service projects related to the river, and study and monitor the ecology of the river. The program reaches some four thousand students each year and is intended to "inspire meaningful personal connection with nature in order to foster a lifelong sense of pride in, belonging to, and stewardship of our natural world."[30]

In Biophilic Cities Citizens Have a Deep Sense of the Natural History of City and Region

In biophilic cities, residents and leaders alike not only understand the present ecological and social conditions but are able to situate that understanding in a deeper arc of history and time. Citizens of a biophilic city are knowledgeable about the geologic and natural history of the city and region, and educating and informing them about this history are key priorities of planning and public policy.

A biophilic city plans and designs with a time frame of hundreds, perhaps thousands of years, rather than with an excessively short-term perspective that often drives decisions. A biophilic city understands the need to consider and appreciate the conditions of life that existed when originally settled as an important point of reference and one guidepost for imagining the fullness and abundance of nature that was and might be possible.

Knowledge of the pre-urban settlement hydrology, or native hydrology, helps frame future commitments to return streams and creeks to the surface and to natural conditions. Historic patterns of biodiversity offer direction and insight about what amount of unique nature and life might be possible in years ahead. In cities like San Francisco, many current planning and design issues are usefully informed by knowledge of the defining geology and ecology of the place. Biophilic cities build their shorter-term plans and policies and projects on the firmer ground of this deeper time and biological history.

In Biophilic Cities Priority Is Placed on Ecological Restoration and Repair

It is remarkable how quickly nature can be restored and revive even the most degraded and hard-surfaced environments. Cities might also be judged on their commitment to restoring and repairing damage done in the past and to actively bringing back nature to urban neighborhoods and centers. In the biophilic cities discussed in this book there are remarkable examples. Vitoria, Spain, for instance, restored its former airport to a world-class and internationally significant wetland park, the Salburua. A major piece of that city's green belt has now become the city's crown jewel of biodiversity and site of a major new nature center that will provide programs and exhibits and space that will help build connections to place and environment.

Restoring nature in cities can happen in the most unusual places, of course, and increasingly in biophilic cities we see new opportunities for greenness. An interesting approach is being taken in Tokyo under a comprehensive ten-year city greening plan. Japanese architect Tadao Ando plans to create a forest in the sea, the Umi-no-Mori or "Sea Forest," by planting trees on an 88-hectare parcel in Tokyo Bay that has served as a landfill for the city since the 1970s. More than 12 million tons of refuse have been deposited on the site. The forest would, among other things, help to enhance the flow of fresh air into the city and would be part of a larger effort to plant nearly a half million new trees and thereby double the number of trees in the city. In addition to the practical ecological and health benefits of this project, Ando has noted the symbolic importance of recycling this site: "The earth is going to face this problem of waste. . . . That's the reason I want to show that waste can be converted into forest. This forest doesn't belong only to Tokyo but to the world."[31] He believes it will become an important symbol of a "recycling society."

We might also judge the measure of a biophilic city in part by the percentage of residents actively involved in one or another form of ecological community building. In every Australian city, for instance, there is an extensive network of citizen groups—often called *urban bushcare*—that results in hundreds, perhaps thousands, of individuals stewarding over often small plots of land in the city, at once socializing and having fun, building friendships, and deepening community commitments while tangibly reconnecting to the earth. Brisbane's program is one of the oldest and largest. Started in 1990, its urban bushcare program, Habitat Brisbane, now consists of 124 different community groups doing restoration work around the

Figure 3.5 Salburua wetlands, part of the greenbelt for the city of Vitoria-Gasteiz in the Basque Country of Spain; this now-international wetland used to be the location of an airport. Photo credit: Tim Beatley

city, involving an estimated 2,500 volunteers.[32] And there are five city staff devoted to helping these Habitat groups, not uncommon across Australian cities (usually at least one bushcare officer, but often several). The goals and objectives of this work are not only conservation and restoration of biodiversity but also education and awareness-raising and community cohesion.[33] Evidence suggests that involvement in urban bushcare and urban restoration work does increase and deepen sense of community.

Biophilic Institutions and Governance

Biophilic cities can also be described by the ways in which they are governed, their funding and budgeting commitments and priorities, and the governance structure and style. How much of a voice is given to biodiversity protection and environmental education, for instance, and how central are the needs of nature in a city's planning and management? How equipped and capable is a city to advance a biophilic agenda?

Biophilic Cities Invest in the Institutions and Infrastructure Necessary to Educate and Foster Connections to Nature, Near and Far

Biophilic cities are to be identified not just by the presence or absence of nature, of greenspaces and green infrastructure, but by other forms of investment that facilitate a biophilic life. A biophilic city invests in a robust network of public and private institutions that will educate urbanites about nature, teach them to restore and protect it, and nudge them toward enjoying nature. These include traditional environmental education and natural science institutions such as local botanical gardens, zoological parks, and natural history museums, among others. Environmental education centers have been very effective in some cities and in some cases are based in urban neighborhoods.

The Cleveland Museum of Natural History works closely with area schools, and in addition to hosting many visits to its exhibit-rich facility (including everything from large dinosaurs to impressive displays of Native American history and heritage of the region), it has native wildlife that it takes to area schools. Members of this local education team include a red-tailed hawk, a groundhog, a skunk, eastern box turtles, and many snakes. There are even arctic hares—native to the northern reaches of the metro Cleveland area—with fur that changes entirely to white as winter approaches. Under the museum's "Adopt-a-Wild Child" program, kids and adults can "adopt" one of the animals, thereby helping to pay for its care and feeding.

The Cleveland Museum is itself an active manager of land and environment in the region, actually holding and conserving some thirty-three preserves, covering some 4,600 acres, under its Natural Areas Program.[34] Increasingly the museum is stepping up to tackle larger local and global environmental challenges and the ecological challenges and opportunities of cities, and it has made space (physical and organizational) for the merging of other agendas and organizations in the region. In 2007, David Beach, who started a local sustainability advocacy group called Eco-City Cleveland, merged this group with the museum, now under the name GreenCityBlueLake Institute. He sees the merger and the museum's move into contemporary urban sustainability matters as a natural extension of their historic mission. The natural history museum is, he believes, the "perfect place to talk about sustainability." "We just have to help them take the leap from thinking about the past, and how life developed, to thinking about the future and what we do with our planet and civilization in the 21st Century. That's the dimension that we [GreenCityBlueLake] bring to the museum."

A number of major U.S. cities have aquariums, which might also rise to fill a more important role in educating about local nature. The National Aquarium in Baltimore views buildings and businesses around the city as potential outposts where educational displays might extend the message of the aquarium. A dramatic example of this can be found in the Barnes and Noble bookstore, in the city's former power plant, just a short walk from the aquarium. At the top of the store's escalator that delivers customers to the second floor is a dramatic and rather large aquarium, teeming with fish. Maintained by the staff of the National Aquarium, this 16-foot, 3,000-gallon tank contains some 1,000 fish and is the result of an unusual partnership between a corporate bookstore and a public institution. The tasks of educating about and fostering connections with nature, as well as conserving and repairing natural systems, can increasingly be understood as a shared endeavor, and biophilic cities look for creative partnerships between public and private entities.

In Vitoria-Gasteiz, Spain, commitment to educating residents about nature has included some unusual investments, including an impressive nature center called Ataria. Located on the edge of the city's Salburua wetlands and connected to its greenbelt and walking trails, the center is a very unusual shape: It juts upward and extends out over the wetlands, providing an unusual vantage on this city's nature. The center is designed as a space to host and stage school visits from around the city and is unusually well equipped.

Figure 3.6 Through an innovative partnership between Barnes and Noble bookstores and the Baltimore aquarium, there is a very large aquarium on the second floor of the B&N bookstore in downtown Baltimore. Customers are drawn to watching the fish. Photo credit: Anneke Bastiaan

Leadership can be provided to ensure that city dwellers have every resource and opportunity to fully enjoy the nature around them. This includes making investments in transit and transit routes that support visitation to key nature areas, as well as in bicycle infrastructure and programs. Cities might also explore extending their usual package of public services in creative ways that entice and facilitate nature and outdoor activities. The municipal library function, for instance, might be extended beyond books to include tents and camping and hiking equipment, as well as canoes and kayaks. Municipal plant nurseries (common in Australia) could grow and distribute native plants, and municipal libraries that lend tools might provide homeowners and neighborhood associations with the equipment and means to convert gray streets and vacant lots into verdant urban spaces.

Biophilic Cities Take Cues from the Larger Environment and Bioregion

A biophilic sensibility or spirit suggests that the city's policies and planning—environmental, housing, and economic development, among others—reflect a consciousness about the unique climate, environment, natural history, and topography, of the bioregion in which its sits. Architecture and building design must take advantage of localized solar and wind and microclimatic conditions, and this will typically help in profoundly reducing energy consumption and heating and cooling needs. Many primary needs, from food production to energy production, can equally build on these bioregional circumstances. What can best be grown, and what is the unique and special food heritage of a city and region? Can the economy of a city be grounded on the unique things that can be made or produced or grown in that special place? Many metropolitan areas have the opportunity, for instance, to nurture local timber production from native species, sustainably managed and harvested, and to eschew wood products traveling from great distances, with questionable provenance and significant environmental impacts.

A commonly cited contrast in sensibilities has often been made between Phoenix and Tucson, Arizona, two cities not far apart and equally situated in a desert ecosystem. Phoenix has largely ignored the unique context, often pretending that its location doesn't matter. Through its profligate use of water and landscaping with water-intensive nonnative species, Phoenix has turned its back on what is special and important—its ecological context and setting. In contrast, Tucson has sought to nurture connections to place, for instance, through the extensive use of native plants in landscaping throughout the public spaces of the city. There is a closeness to and sensitivity about the desert landscape and its flora and fauna that is largely missing in Phoenix. Neither city is a perfect story, to be sure, but the contrast suggests how central bioregion can be.

The cities of the U.S. Northwest and British Columbia reflect a similar sensibility about bioregional context, with many efforts at planning and policy that build on this unique setting. A Northwest organization, EcoTrust, has developed the idea of "Salmon Nation" as a unifying label and moniker for this region—suggesting that places where free-running salmon can be found are more alike than different, the basis for bioregional commonality and identity.

A biophilic city and region resist the tendencies toward globalized sameness, understanding that the ecology and wildlife, climate and weather, and natural history and culture will be profoundly different from one place to another.

Biophilic Cities Work to Protect Nature beyond Their Borders

Each city has opportunities to express care about the environment and other life in the world. Large cities exert a tremendous pressure on global biodiversity through their material flows and consumption patterns, and one measure of a biophilic city is the extent to which it seeks to moderate or reduce those impacts.

Some cities have taken steps to ban plastic grocery bags, for instance, responsible, by some estimates, for the death of some 100,000 marine mammals.[35] San Francisco has become the first American city to impose such a ban. Another step might be stemming the tide of tropical hardwoods coming into a city or region, much of it illegally harvested and having significant impacts on biodiversity.

New York City, for instance, has recently acknowledged that it purchases a large amount of tropical hardwoods, an estimated $1 million worth each year. The city uses this wood—South American species such as *Ipe* and *Garapa*—for such things as benches, boardwalks, and ferry landings. The ten-mile-long Brooklyn Bridge Promenade is constructed of greenheart (*Chlorocardium rodiei*), another South American hardwood. In recognition of the destructive impact of such purchases Mayor Bloomberg announced a plan in 2008 to significantly reduce the city's purchasing of such wood—a 20 percent reduction immediately and larger reductions later as the city researches and pilots alternative wood sources and alternative materials that could be used.[36] Describing tropical deforestation as an "ecological calamity" and noting that it may be responsible for as much as 20 percent of greenhouse gas emissions, Mayor Bloomberg has made an eloquent plea for cities to become better stewards of the global environment. "New Yorkers don't live in the rain forest. But we do live in a world that we all share. And we're committed to doing everything we can to protect it for all of our children."[37] City purchasing policies and decisions are important opportunities for biophilic values to gain expression.[38]

While living in Western Australia I was impressed with the actions taken at both governmental and individual levels to protect and nurture the unique marine life in this state with an immense ocean shoreline. Our home for about four months was the charming former whaling port of Fremantle, near Perth. Despite this city's whaling past, or in some measure because of it, it has emerged as a champion for whales and other marine life.

The mayor, Peter Tagliaferri, has taken steps to make the city's current anti-whaling position clear. Most impressively, the city has made it clear that Japanese whaling vessels are not welcome in its port, and the mayor has sent letters to Indonesian port cities asking them to take similar action.

While cities are not commonly party to international agreements or treaties, it is true that some cities are able to undertake conservation and protection actions based on partnership agreements that are treaty-like and to acknowledge a commitment to biodiversity and nature that extends beyond their borders. The U.S. Fish and Wildlife Agency created in 1999 an interesting partnership mechanism that provides cities with the chance to give meaning to these values. Called the Urban Conservation Treaty for Migratory Birds, the program provides small matching grants for participating cities, to support conservation and education efforts. These are cities located along flyways or with large amounts of migratory bird habitats, such as New Orleans, the first participating city, which has some 23,000 acres of national wildlife refuge (the Bayou Sauvage) within its city limits. Other participating American cities include Philadelphia, Chicago, and Houston.[39]

Care for nature and other forms of life in (and beyond) the biophilic city can be expressed in many different ways. It can be seen in the adoption of bird-friendly design standards to minimize loss of bird life, both migratory and local species, from tall buildings in the city (see chapter 2). It can be seen in the efforts in some cities to build wildlife underpasses and overpasses and to generally guide growth and design development to minimize impact on biodiversity of local and global significance.

The sensibility of care for other species, local and global, can also be seen through efforts at ecological repair and restoration. With the rise in importance given to green infrastructure in recent years, many cities are making an effort to enhance and restore the ecological and hydrologic systems that define those places at a regional and bioregional level. Many American cities have sought to repair and restore rivers and to reestablish physical connections and connectedness to them. New efforts are under way, for instance, to restore natural functions of the Los Angeles River. Currently more a concrete flood channel than natural system, it touches virtually every neighborhood in that city, and an ambitious new urban design holds real potential to enhance the living conditions of thousands of residents. Perhaps most boldly, the city of Seoul, South Korea took down some four miles of an elevated freeway to allow access to the Cheonggyecheon River, which had been hidden beneath it. This was a campaign pledge of then-mayor Lee Myung-bak, now president of South Korea, demonstrating that bold actions on behalf of the biophilic city need not be a political liability.

And the restorative work of cities like Los Angeles and Seoul demonstrate and help to advance a global ethic of caring about nature and environment and show the importance of global leadership on these issues.

Concluding Thoughts

What constitutes a biophilic city is still very much a matter of discussion and debate. Less a definitive list or set of principles, the categories described are meant to identify at least some of the potential building blocks of a biophilic city. It is unlikely that a singular coherent vision of a biophilic city will emerge. Rather, perhaps there are many different kinds of biophilic cities, many different expressions of urban biophilia. And they might be expressed by different combinations and emphases of the qualities and conditions described here. At the simplest level, though, a biophilic city is a city that seeks to foster a closeness to nature—it protects and nurtures what it has (understands that abundant wild nature is important), actively restores and repairs the nature that exists, while finding new and creative ways to insert and inject nature into the streets, buildings, and urban living environments. And a biophilic city is an outdoor city, a city that makes walking and strolling and daily exposure to the outside elements and weather possible and a priority.

But as the above discussion also indicates, a biophilic city is not just about physical conditions or natural setting, and it is not just about green design and ecological interventions—it is just as much about a city's underlying biophilic spirit and sensibilities, about its funding priorities, and about the importance it places on support for programs that entice urbanites to learn more about the nature around them, for instance. A biophilic city might be measured and assessed more by how curious its citizens are about the nature around them and the extent to which they are engaged in daily activities to enjoy and care for nature than by the physical qualities or conditions or, for instance, the number or acres of parks and greenspaces per capita that exist in a city.

Four

Biophilic Urban Design and Planning

Natural and biophilic elements need to be central in everything and anything we design and build, from schools and hospitals to neighborhoods and urban blocks, to street systems and larger urban- and regional-scale design and planning. The discussion in this chapter focuses on four primary scales: the region, the city, the neighborhood, and the building. The type and extent of natural features will vary in part depending on the scale of attention (see box 4.1).

I begin with a discussion of the region because from a spatial and ecological perspective it sets the larger stage in which many of the other biophilic design ideas and planning strategies can be applied. It is the larger canvas, if you will, and an important strategy in its own right. A "rooftop to region" or "room to region" approach is needed. The best biophilic cities are places where these different scales overlap and reinforce biophilic behaviors and lifestyles—children or adults should be able to leave their front door and move through a series of green features and biophilic elements, moving if they choose from garden and courtyard to green street and municipal forest and then to larger expanses of regional nature. Ideally, in a biophilic city these scales work together to deliver a nested nature that is more than the sum of its parts.

There are a number of different green and biophilic design ideas, features, initiatives, and projects to cite, far more than just a decade or two ago. The challenges to planners, designers, and policymakers to integrate nature into our daily urban lives and propel adults and children outside remain serious, but we do not lack sufficient precedent and a stock of test ideas and techniques.

There is an extensive biophilic design palette, and what follows is a more detailed discussion of these tools and some positive and compelling examples of how they have been applied and put into practice.

Box 4.1
Biophilic Urban Design Elements across Scales

Scale   *Biophilic Design Elements*

Building   Green rooftops
                            Sky gardens and green atria
                            Rooftop garden
                            Green walls
                            Daylit interior spaces

Block   Green courtyards
                            Clustered housing around green areas
                            Native species yards and spaces

Street   Green streets
                            Sidewalk gardens
                            Urban trees
                            Low-impact development
                            Vegetated swales and skinny streets
                            Edible landscaping
                            High degree of permeability

Neighborhood   Stream daylighting, stream restoration
                            Urban forests
                            Ecology parks
                            Community gardens
                            Neighborhood parks and pocket parks
                            Greening grayfields and brownfields

Community   Urban creeks and riparian areas
                            Urban ecological networks
                            Green schools
                            City tree canopy
                            Community forest and community orchards
                            Greening utility corridors

Region   River systems and floodplains
                            Riparian systems
                            Regional greenspace systems
                            Greening major transport corridors

Source: Modified from Girling and Kellett, first appeared in Beatley, 2008.

Green Regions and Compact Cities

At regional, bioregional, or metropolitan levels, importance must be given to preserving and restoring large interconnected green systems—forests, rivers and riparian networks, farmlands—that create the larger template in which green systems at smaller scales fit. Regional- and urban-scale green networks serve many functions, including climate modification and urban heat island mitigation (German cities protect forested riparian areas because of the positive movement of fresh air through urban areas), habitat conservation, water quality protection, carbon sequestration, and sustainable wood production, but providing recreational benefits and access to nature for urban residents is a major goal. Compact, dense cities lay the foundation for biophilic living and biophilic regional planning in several important ways. Compact urban form holds the potential to profoundly reduce the amount of land consumed and the impact on regional ecosystems, while expanding access to the green infrastructure and larger expanses of nature in which cities lie.

Compactness and density create the conditions in which walking and daily outside living become more possible. As writer David Owen argues in his book *Green Metropolis*, Manhattan represents an important model for future sustainable living because its density creates the conditions for walkability. "A resident of a dense city almost can't help logging at least an hour or two outside every day, just doing things like walking to work, walking to lunch, walking to the subway, and walking to perform various errands."[1] A livelier, more active mixed-use street will make walking easier and may even change the perception of distance; walking trips will feel shorter, more manageable, and more enjoyable. "Going outside is actually a more normal, ordinary activity in a dense city," says Owen, "because there it's an indivisible element of daily life."[2]

There is a long tradition, particularly in Europe, of planning regional ecological networks and guiding regional planning to ensure the existence of and access to these larger networks. In German, Dutch, and Scandinavian cities, for instance, importance has been given to bringing about compact urban form, often along transit lines, but within a large regional network of greenspaces that in many cases come into the very center of cities.[3] In Copenhagen, its famous regional "fingers" plan, with large green wedges that extend from the center to outlying areas of nature, dates to 1947. In Helsinki, large green wedges have similarly been designed. Keskuspuisto, Helsinki's Central Park, is one of the best examples of regional greenspace planning—it extends 11 kilometers from old-growth forest at the city's edge to the center of this compact, fairly dense city. In green urban cities, greenspace and natural landscape should be in close proximity to where dense populations exist and should be easily reachable by public transit. In Hannover, Germany, an 80-kilometer-long "green ring" has recently been completed, connecting very large blocks of greenspace and a diverse set of ecosystems that surround the city. In this city, the network includes a large (and beautiful) 650-hectare forest, the Eilenriede, in its very center.

Spanish cities, historically dense and compact, have managed at once to contain growth at a regional level and to conserve and protect large green areas close to where most people live. Vitoria-Gasteiz is an excellent case in point. Located in the Basque country of northern Spain, this city of 250,000 illustrates both the virtues of compact dense cities and the value of a regional approach. Vitoria is truly a pedestrian city, a city whose dense and compact form fosters a physically active, outdoor life. The numbers tell it all: Nearly 50 percent of all trips made in the municipality of Vitoria-Gasteiz are made on foot (yes, you read that correctly). And this statistic applies not just to the city center but the entire region, as the boundaries of the municipality encompass not only the city but much of the surrounding region (a very useful planning circumstance). There are plenty of cars in Vitoria, and the percentage of trips by car is on the rise as walking trips decline compared with a decade ago, so there are certainly challenges to confront. But overall this is a walking city, a city where one spends a great portion of the day outdoors and out of cars.

In Vitoria, there are no tall skyscrapers but rather dense blocks of housing, six to ten stories high, with restaurants, shops, and bars on the street level, extensive public spaces, and a vibrant urban life. And there is very little of the usual low-density suburban residential development. This compact, land-efficient urban form makes it a city of short distances. And it is surrounded by an immense network of nature and rural land, much of it easily accessible by foot from the center of the city. There has been an extensive effort, over a number of years, at creating a greenbelt—a connected network of greenspaces and natural habitat that circles the city. Six major parks are now connected in the greenbelt, which is approximately 600 hectares (about 1,500 acres) and on the way to being 1,000 hectares (about 2,400 acres).

Other Spanish cities are even denser and more compact. Barcelona is frequently heralded for its compactness and many efforts to enhance and improve urban livability. Overall Barcelona boasts nearly 15,000 inhabitants per square kilometer, and in the Gràcia district, where residents have access to extensive green areas, the density approaches 30,000 persons per square kilometer, rivaling the density of almost any global city. And in part because of this dense urban form, Barcelona and the Barcelona region boast impressive greenspaces, including Collserola Park, an 8,000-hectare park (about 20,000 acres) only a few minutes travel time from the downtown, containing "10 million trees, 1,000 different species of plants and close to 190 species of vertebrates."[4]

In Vitoria, many of the greenspaces around the city have been ecologically reclaimed and restored, notably Salburúa Park, a gem in the Vitoria system. Once a municipal airport, the site is now a reclaimed and internationally significant wetland. A visit to Salburúa shows just how close the park is to much of the new development. The park is a major amenity for these residents, and real estate developers are beginning to understand its potential and include proximity to the park in advertising and marketing materials. In Armentia Park, an element of the southern part of the greenbelt, a major road has been placed underground to create a land bridge and physical connection to this large park for pedestrians. The Spanish effectively tie together the natural with the history and cultural heritage of their cities. One of the wonderful ways this has been done in Vitoria is by connecting the mountaintops in the region with a walking trail. Called the Shepherd's Route, the trail connects large blocks of biodiversity and highlights the region's ancient agricultural practices and past.

With the success of the first ring of the greenbelt, Vitoria has been working hard to imagine and develop an outer ring of nature and to connect these inner and outer greenbelts. The province of Alava contains immense biodiversity, much of it already in some form of protective category, and the new vision for the future is to connect and extend the city's pedestrian trails and network to these larger blocks of land and habitat. And the nature not far from the center of Vitoria is immense and quite wild, given how long it has been inhabited. One of gems in the regional network is Gorbeia Park, some 20,000 hectares (nearly 50,000 acres) and home to diverse wildlife, including wild boar, badgers, and even Iberian wolves. This is found just a little over twenty kilometers from the center of Vitoria.

Other cities have pursued similar visions of compact urban form and regional greenspace networks that will efficiently preserve and link green infrastructure while creating easy opportunities for urbanities to hike or stroll or bike. Many American cities have developed urban trail systems that provide tremendous recreational opportunities with the chance to get close to nature. The trail network in Anchorage, Alaska is one of the more notable examples, partly because this relatively small American city (a population of around 300,000) has so much native wildness remaining within its boundaries. The city has also conserved more than 11,000 acres of parkland and greenspace within its borders, a remarkable accomplishment.

Canadian cities offer similar lessons about how to combine greenness and density and to stimulate outdoor, physically active lives. The Vancouver metropolitan regional growth strategy emphasizes the conservation of nature and farmland. The city of Vancouver is designed to be compact, walkable, and transit accessible (the SkyTrain). Much of the new urban development has been guided to high-rise structures. The City of Vancouver adopted an "eco-density charter" in 2008, further emphasizing the importance and desirability of increased density in the city.[5] This is part of Mayor Gregor Robertson's plan to make Vancouver the greenest city in the world. This high-density livable city is biophilic, from the ubiquitous spectacular views of the surrounding mountains, to Stanley Park that makes up the peninsula of the city, to the city's extensive waterfront and seawall promenade.

Compact urban form and land conservation must also be accompanied by efforts to overcome habitat fragmentation. The Brisbane, Australia metro region represents another exemplary effort to contain growth and conserve large areas of nature at a regional level (through its South East Queensland Regional Plan) and also to protect extensive biodiversity in and around the city. The city of Brisbane has been a leader and has identified a Core Biodiversity Network, emphasizing biological corridors and giving priority to projects that facilitate wildlife movement and connectivity throughout the city. I had the chance to visit one of the most impressive early efforts here in the construction of a multispecies "fauna-friendly crossing structure." Built in 2004, it includes a two-arched land bridge with native trees and vegetation to facilitate animal movements, as well as a series of eight-meter-high glider poles (resting and launching poles for species such as the squirrel glider), rope ladders (canopy bridges), fauna underpasses and culverts (e.g., for movement of amphibians), and exclusion fencing to steer animals to these crossing points. A study of the effectiveness of the crossing structures by the Center for Innovative Conservation Strategies at Griffith University found that they did in fact work, resulting in significant reduction in roadkill.[6] Recent concerns about the long-range and very serious potential impacts of climate change have provided even more support for Brisbane's strategy of corridors and connections, including Brisbane Forest Park, which includes a significant altitudinal range that will permit some species to adapt to changing climate.[7]

Parks, Trees, and Urban Forests

Having parks within a certain distance of where people live is important if we want residents to use them and to walk to them. Researchers sometimes talk of the problem of "distance decay," the quite understandable effect that if parks are too far away, frequency of their use will drop off. Research shows that "distance decay is in all instances characterized by a steep decline in use frequency with increasing distance, especially over the first 100–300 m." "In conditions of good access (<100 m) the use frequency is more evenly distributed among the residents (at a high level). Given poorer access conditions (>100 m) a smaller fraction of the residents seem to maintain high use frequencies but the majority uses the parks substantially less compared to good access conditions."[8]

Providing a degree of wildness in cities, an important biophilic goal, suggests new thinking about parks, and these spaces should be more than turfgrass and benches and the standard play equipment. One recent example of a different kind of park can be seen in Teardrop Park, in the Battery Park neighborhood of New York City. This example shows that parks in the city, even very small ones, can be wild and natural. Here a two-acre parcel, sandwiched between several buildings, including the new green residential high-rise Solaire, has been designed by landscape architect Michael Van Valkenburg to include a variety of natural habitats that might be found in the Hudson River Valley.

Some 88 percent of the vegetation planted is in the form of native species (almost 17,000 plants in total), and there are hills and interesting topography to stimulate nature play. There are a number of other ecological features: A rainwater barrel collects water for the lawns, trees and shrubs are watered from blackwater from the Soltaire, and stone and other materials were sourced from with five hundred miles of the site. A large rock wall is one of the most special elements of this park. Climbable in the summer, in the winter it sports a frozen cascade of ice, with a clever water system that recirculates water in the summer and creates an ice wall in the winter.

Trees and urban forests represent additional opportunities for reinserting nature into cities. And it is a matter of not only increasing the presence of nature but providing significant economic benefits to urban communities as well. A mature hardwood tree can provide, for example, the equivalent air-conditioning benefits, through evapotranspiration, of ten room-sized air-conditioning units, operating twenty hours per day. Trees and forests provide shade, retain stormwater, reduce ozone pollution, and add economic value to property.[9]

Figure 4.1 Teardrop Park, NYC. Photo credit: Tim Beatley

Planting trees and urban forests is another essential step in greening the city and a helpful form of urban nature. Most cities have some form of urban forestry program, and recently a number of cities have set ambitious tree planting targets. Both Los Angeles and New York City have set the goal of planting a million new trees. Even Houston has set a million-tree goal under the leadership of its popular green mayor, Bill White.

Australian cities have been even more ambitious—the city of Brisbane has initiated a campaign to plant 2 million new trees in that (hot) city by 2012. Brisbane's local growth management strategy envisions a "canopy of shade" extending across the city.[10]

However, in many U.S. cities tree cover is in decline, both in central city and inner-suburban areas through mortality and insufficient tree replacement and in suburbanizing areas through careless land clearance. Atlanta is a case in point. According to analysis by American Forests, tree coverage for the Atlanta metro area declined from 45 percent in 1974 to only 29 percent, in 2001.[11] In a widely cited study, the Washington, D.C. region saw a 64 percent decline in tree cover between 1973 and 1997.[12] In response, many cities have now adopted some form of urban tree conservation and planting initiative. Largely in response to the good work of American Forests, based in Washington, D.C. (and analysis through their CITY green software), many cities now have a better idea of changing tree canopy over time, and many have adopted the American Forests–advocated goal of 40 percent coverage.[13]

A recent assessment of urban tree canopy coverage for the city of Baltimore found the present coverage to be only 20 percent. Through analysis of sites in the city where additional planting could occur in the future, it has been estimated that tree canopy coverage of more than 70 percent is possible.[14] In Los Angeles the urban canopy is at 18 percent, with even fewer trees to be found in many of the city's least-advantaged neighborhoods. In Sacramento, more than 400,000 trees have been planted since 1990 through the initiative of SMUD, the Sacramento Municipal Utility District.[15] This especially progressive utility recognizes that tree planting and distribution of free trees is more than paid for through reductions in summer cooling demands.

The Philadelphia metro area has seen similar reductions in tree canopy coverage (an 8% decline over the last fifteen years[16]), and the Pennsylvania Horticultural Society has been actively encouraging and facilitating tree planting in that city. Specifically, it runs a neighborhood-based program called Tree Tenders, in which citizens go through nine hours of training to learn how to tend and care for street trees planted in their neighborhoods.[17]

Much can be done to restore and regrow urban forests, and clearly there is much more room for trees and forests in cities. We should also look for new ways to include edible species, especially in the existing city parks and municipal properties. Recent examples include the George Washington Carver Edible Park in Asheville, North Carolina and the Orchard School Park in Cleveland, Ohio, illustrating the potential for planting fruit trees in the often underused spaces around schools (and helping to feed neighborhoods and build food resilience at the same time). In other cities there are examples of municipal woodlots and community forests that are often harvested and become an important element in helping move a city and region in the direction of local economy and shortened supply lines.[18]

Reimagining the Interstices of the City

The very spaces around and between the buildings and streets in a city represent many other opportunities to inject and insert natural wildness. If there is any nature at all in these spaces it is often turfgrass or mowed spaces,

Figure 4.2
Jane Martin, who founded
the organization
PLANT★SF, in front of
new sidewalk gardens in
the Mission District in San
Francisco, California.
Photo credit: Tim Beatley

not especially wild or biophilic. Yet side yards and backyards and urban strips of land of various kinds could be places for the most creative urban nature interventions.

A significant challenge in dense urban environments is to reimagine the many existing hard surfaces as opportunities to insert green life. In San Francisco, recent years have witnessed the conversion of a number of barren and hard-surface sidewalks into green oases. Much of this conversion can be attributed to the leadership and tutelage of Jane Martin, often referred to as "the woman who can operate a jackhammer," for her persistent efforts to take up hard surface roadway and sidewalk space and to create green, permeable spaces in their stead. In 2004 she started the nonprofit PLANT★SF, which stands for "Permeable Landscape as Neighborhood Treasure." A practicing architect, Martin and her firm, Shift Design Studio, have done some of the most creative urban greening designs in San Francisco.

Martin's projects can be found throughout the city now, but many of the early examples can be seen in her home neighborhood, the Mission District. This is an especially good place to test out these de-sealing strategies as most of the residential sidewalks are unusually wide—at least fifteen feet and sometimes as wide as twenty feet. The results of her creative insertion of green are really sidewalk gardens; in some cases, green vegetated features on both sides of the sidewalk create a kind of linear sidewalk park.

One of her first projects, around the corner from her Harrison Street office and home in the Mission District, is the conversion of a barren sidewalk extension (a "bulb-out") actually created a number of years ago in an effort to better control cars, create new pedestrian spaces, and civilize these car-dominated spaces. But the result was not a very green or natural setting. So Martin was able to activate the neighborhood and proposed to dramatically green these spaces. She has done so very impressively. The curb extension is now a small neighborhood green with a great variety of plants, some donated by residents of the neighborhood. This project has served as a catalyst for another five neighborhoods to start their own series of sidewalk interventions. Altogether more than two thousand square feet of paved surface was replaced with flowers, grasses, and trees and their accompanying beautiful hues, scents, and insect life.

The PLANT*SF work demonstrates the variety of different ways that green, permeable features can be inserted into the city. It has been opening up planting wells close to building walls (a "living buffer"), installing clinging plants and vines on walls and fences, de-sealing portions of driveways to create green planting strips, and of course planting trees. Mostly native plants are used in these projects, and in some cases the plantings are edible.

That San Francisco needs these green and permeable projects is now increasingly clear. It is a highly paved city, with a significant flooding and CSO (combined sewer overflow) problem. Martin tells the wrenching story of the flooding a few years ago that resulted in raw sewage backing up through her bathroom pipes and covering the floors of her home. There is a growing recognition of the value of things such as green rooftops, rain barrels (the city only recently changed its codes to allow homeowners to disconnect their downspouts), and low-impact development, and the sidewalk parks and greening that Martin advocates fall well into this new support.

The social results are also considerable here, as Martin reports on the PLANT*SF Web site: "In addition to the environmental benefits, this

project [Harrison street green] has resulted in a significant social transformation of the block—reinforcing the pedestrian scale, making a more
hospitable and interesting walking experience, and inviting neighborly in-
teractions. The plantings have brought together long time residents with
more recent arrivals—as evidenced by neighbors introducing themselves
after 30 years of living around the corner from each other and a 4-day-old
introduced to nature on his first outing."[19] The social value of these greening projects, and the ability to bind people to a neighborhood and to each
other, is clear in simply walking around the Mission District with Martin—
she seems to know everyone.

PLANT★SF helps promote urban greening in a number of ways,
including through pilot and demonstration projects, public education and
awareness raising, the publishing of useful technical materials for neighborhoods (and designers), such as a set of online plant selection guidelines, and
of course advocacy.

Martin's advocacy work has led to some especially significant
changes to city policy, making it easier to gain city approval for sidewalk
gardens. She has actually been able to get the City of San Francisco to create a new kind of permit (a "sidewalk landscaping permit"), making the
permit process less burdensome and costly and generally less of an obstacle
to greening neighborhoods. The cost of the permit even goes down with
the number of neighboring property owners who sign on.[20] There have
now been some five hundred of these permits issued for sidewalk gardens
and greening projects throughout the city, and so Martin has been successful
at setting in motion a new way of looking at dense urban neighborhoods in
that city and perhaps setting a model for other cities to follow.

Finding space for new parks in already dense cities is a challenge,
and again creative thinking about what a park is becomes necessary. In Paris,
one of the more unusual locations for a park is found on the top of a dis-
used elevated railway line. Created in 2000 and known as the Promenade
Plantée (the planted promenade), this linear park—with trees, greenery, and
benches—kind of floats above the city. The elevated portion of the park, or
the viaduct, is about 1.5 kilometers in length, and the entire park encom-
passes about 4.5 kilometers in length. The park begins from just south of
the Bastille Opera House, connecting to Reuilly Garden. Occasional stair-
way access is provided to the street level below, where one can find shops
and offices created from the viaduct structure itself. The elevated portions
snake their way alongside apartment buildings and actually through several
buildings.

So impressive has the Promenade Plantée been that it has served as
the inspiration to the High Line, a similar park and urban green project in

New York City. Here, an elevated freight line from the 1930s runs through the Chelsea district of Manhattan and has been the center of a multiyear effort to save and creatively reuse this structure as an elevated garden and walking park.[21] When completed, it will create a unique elevated green park, connecting every few blocks with the surface streets below. The first segment of the park has been completed and is heavily used.[22]

Other dense cities are also exploring new and creative ways to insert nature into the urban fabric. Barcelona's Agency for Urban Ecology, for instance, has released an ambitious plan and vision for the future of the city that envisions even more nature there, and in particular new green elements in the interior of the dense city. What is imagined is an interconnected network of parks and greenspaces. *Intervias,* or interior courtyards of superblocks in the city, would be converted to green oases. Barcelona is a city of mostly flat roofs, and this new vision imagines an "elevated green network" of green rooftops and rooftop gardens, a "green mantle" that "would form a green zone connecting areas such as Collserola, Tres Turons and Monjuic, which are currently disconnected."[23]

A River Runs Through It (the City, That Is)

Every American city represents a highly altered urban hydrology. Often the presence of a river, or confluence of several rivers, is the major historical reason a city exists where it does, but too often the river's edge habitats have been degraded or destroyed, its water quality and other aquatic values have been compromised, and the city has physically turned its back to the river. This has changed in the last several decades as many cities have rediscovered their rivers and taken impressive steps to restore and reconnect to them. Portland, Oregon; Milwaukee; San Jose; Denver; and Washington, D.C., among others, have undertaken ambitious river restoration efforts.

Few stories of restoring urban waters are as arousing, or as seemingly herculean, as the efforts to bring back the ancient Cheonggyecheon creek that runs through the center of Seoul, South Korea. A tributary of the Han River, its stock rose with the campaign for mayor of Lee Myung-bak (now president of South Korea), who pledged to restore it. The mayor did the seemingly impossible and took down the elevated highway and brought back to the surface six kilometers (about four miles) of the creek, making it an urban amenity unparalleled in that city and a focal point of pedestrian life. Along with the creek itself, the city has invested in many other design elements: several new pedestrian bridges across the river, stepping-stones in places that let pedestrians cross the river, new fountains, and murals and artwork of various kinds. It has been a tremendous success, with some ninety thousand pedestrians now visiting the river each day.[24] And ecologically it has been a success as well, substantially enhancing the ecosystem and bio-diversity, as well as the overall environmental health of the city (e.g., en-hancing air quality as a result).

Even for the most degraded urban rivers and streams, there is potential for rebirth and for reconnecting urban populations to this natural hydrology. The possibilities for a green renewal of the Los Angeles River and for bringing nature to many of the city's neighborhoods are huge. This waterway currently passes thirty-two miles through L.A., with most neigh-borhoods physically (and emotionally) cut off from it. Even those occupy-ing homes and buildings a few feet away find difficulty reaching the river. And most of the river is presently in the form of a concrete-lined canal, not very attractive or natural over most of its course.

Efforts are under way to change these conditions, however, and in 2007 an impressive Los Angeles River Revitalization Master Plan was de-veloped. Strongly supported by Los Angeles mayor Antonio Villaraigosa, the vision laid here is bold indeed: viewing the river as an opportunity to green neighborhoods, retain continuous riparian habitat, create new parks and points of public access, and become a venue and focus for new suitable rein-vestment, among other elements.[25]

About two hundred miles to the north of Los Angeles is the much smaller city of San Luis Obispo, which has its own story of rediscovering urban water. Here the ecologically significant San Luis Creek runs through its downtown. Several years ago there were plans to fill in and pave over a portion of this creek to create more downtown parking. That threat was beaten back and also served to renew the city's appreciation for this amaz-ing water resource that passes though the town. The city has since invested in a number of public facilities that enhance access to the creek, including a series of walkways that will take residents and visitors down to the water, an outdoor amphitheater, and a very dramatic pedestrian bridge that spans the creek. The city's merchants have also rediscovered the creek, with new out-door seating areas that overlook the creek, for instance, and they now see the creek as an economic amenity for downtown businesses, not just some-thing hidden and forgotten.

In Richmond, Virginia, there is a new appreciation for the James River, which bisects that city and its downtown on its way to the Chesa-peake Bay. The river has, as in many American cities, been largely forgotten, and many obstacles have been erected to make it difficult to reach the river. Many of the city's main downtown streets simply don't reach the river, and over the years the location of heavy industries, floodwalls, and other infra-

Figure 4.3 A segment of the Los Angeles River, showing both the highly engineered aspect and some of the nature that can still be found. Photo credit: Tim Beatley

structural elements of the city have served to create almost insurmountable obstacles. But that is changing, and a major plank in the city's new Downtown Plan is rediscovering the river, making it more accessible to residents, and indeed viewing the river as the city's "great wet Central Park."[26] The plan identifies a number of interesting and creative new ways to reconnect the city to its most prominent natural feature, including creating new tree-lined green street connections (10th Street will connect the State Capitol to the river), purchasing and protecting some of the existing privately owned islands, and building new pedestrian bridges, walking trails, and promenades along the river. Another key goal expressed in the plan is the need to protect views of and visual access to the river.

The Richmond plan also proposes new height limitations on construction along the river to ensure these historic views are not lost. The plan also envisions new parks and recreational space among the islands of the river, converting former industrial land to park and recreational uses. Already this network of islands serves as a wild oasis, not far from the center of the city. Belle Isle is viewed by the city as a wilderness park and provides visitors, kids and adults alike, an unusual opportunity to romp on the rocky and watery expansiveness of the James.

A number of American communities have now undertaken projects to "daylight" creeks and streams—that is, to bring them back to the surface, to restore them to some degree of natural condition or functioning. Richard Pinkham[27] was able to identify more than fifty daylighting projects, the earliest beginning in the early 1980s (Strawberry Creek in Berkeley), and the number continues to expand. The result can be truly spectacular, as in the case of daylighting a segment of Charlottesville's Meadow Creek, through my own University of Virginia. Here, an invisible segment of the creek, in an underground pipe, has been returned to the surface and restored as an amazingly biodiverse habitat, now teeming with invertebrate and bird life. As Pinkham notes, in addition to the ecological and aesthetic benefits, daylighting can actually be a cost-effective action when the need exists to replace undersized culverts. And the potential improvements in quality of life and reconnections to nature are tremendous.

There has been a significant rethinking of stormwater management in many American cities, with some promising results. A number of cities faced with problems of flooding, water quality impacts of urban runoff, and combined sewer overflow are taking steps to retain stormwater on site through a variety of specific techniques now commonly referred to as low-impact development (or LID). Low-impact development (more on this below) argues for the need for a robust network of smaller stormwater retention and treatment facilities, and LID projects have gained much favor and many new supporters in recent years. LID includes many of the greening techniques already mentioned in this chapter, including green rooftops, rain gardens and bioswales, urban tree planting, and permeable paving. Low-impact development originated in the U.S. east coast (Prince Georges County, Maryland) but has now been embraced by cities around the country.

Biophilic Streets and Infrastructure

Biophilic urban design at the neighborhood (and city) level also requires profound rethinking about infrastructure and infrastructural needs. The Western Harbor project in Malmö, Sweden, for instance, turns the power grid on its head—energy infrastructure here is in the form of resilient on-site production, restorative and renewable. Roads, bridges, tunnels, ports, to name a few, could all be profoundly reconceived and reimagined through a biophilic lens. The so-called green bridge in London, for instance, connects two pieces of an otherwise fractured ecology park, almost like a magic green carpet of mature trees and greenery (and no cars) floating above several lanes of congested urban traffic. A sewage treatment plant in Seattle has become (partly) a park and hiking trail, while a recycling facility in Phoenix has been redefined as an opportunity to teach about waste—there are increasingly many good examples to be found.[28]

Streets must be reconceived as not only (or primarily) infrastructure for the conveyance of cars and traffic but as places that harbor native plants and biodiversity, that collect and treat stormwater, and where pedestrians can experience intimate contact with nature as part of their daily routine. The rise in the use of LID techniques to address stormwater (mentioned above) has provided new opportunities to profoundly rethink yards, streets, and alleys. In Seattle, for example, under the leadership of the Seattle Public Utility, an effort has been made to show the natural alternatives to conventional street, sidewalk, and yard designs, demonstrating LID methods through the retrofitting of existing streets. Beginning with its Street Edge Alternatives program, wide auto-dominated (suburban) streets have been converted into narrow, wavy, vegetation-filled green streets, with sidewalks. There is now a seemingly endless diversity of wildflowers and greenery. The street has become a series of rain gardens collecting and treating stormwater and nourishing this verdant scene, where sterile, conventional turfgrass laws existed for the most part before. Seattle has now gone beyond converting single streets to creating entire "green grids" of connecting and intersecting roadways that together set the baseline condition for these green neighborhoods.

Evidence suggests that these LID systems are highly effective at containing the stormwater and controlling urban pollutants, and of course enhancing the amenity (and economic) value of urban neighborhoods. Portland, Oregon is also implementing an extensive green initiative, inserting low-impact development techniques, such a bioswales and rain gardens, along streets and sidewalks and using curb extensions as opportunities to collect and retain stormwater on site. Already some five hundred of these green street stormwater interventions have been undertaken, and many more are on the way in that city.

The city of Sydney, Australia, for instance, released a sustainability plan that calls for a network of "green transformers"—compact facilities that produce power through combined heating, cooling, and power technology, collect stormwater and wastewater, extract biogas for energy production, and provide a surface-level park for the neighborhood.[29] This kind of multifunctional view of the infrastructure in our cities can increasingly be seen to have both economic and ecological advantages.

City leaders and those who plan and design their built environments will need to think much more creatively about water in the years ahead, seeking new forms of urban infrastructure that collect, treat, and reuse this water in novel ways. Chicago architects Sarah Dunn and Martin Felsen of the studio UrbanLab have put forth an interesting new vision for water that profoundly reimagines conventional infrastructure. Dubbed

"Growing Water," their concept envisions a network of fifty "eco-boulevards" running from the west of the city to Lake Michigan. This new network of green ribbons would collect stormwater and create a "living machine" to treat wastewater in the city. In turn, the eco-boulevards represent new greenspace in the city and would end in the west in larger "terminal parks," again rethinking the very nature of a park. Under this bold proposal the city of Chicago would be "re-engineered as a living system."[30]

The city of Chicago has also created an interesting Green Alley Program, intended to retrofit over time its nineteen hundred miles of alleys. Permeable paving (reducing flooding and allowing stormwater to percolate into the ground), rain gardens and bioswales and rain barrels, use of lighter paving materials that are more reflective (and thus help to cool the urban environment), and new energy-efficient and dark sky–friendly lighting fixtures are all part of this rethinking of alleys (the city has prepared a Green Alley Handbook to help promote these ideas). Already much greening has already occurred, and work is under way on some twenty alleys in city.[31] In Baltimore a number of urban alleyways have now been converted to green gathering spaces under a unique new program and local ordinance that makes this possible.

Food and Agriculture in the City

Much understandable new attention is being paid to where our food comes from, its carbon and environmental footprint, and how healthful it is. There is a growing movement to produce and process more of our food locally, and there is a great opportunity for cities to be more food resilient and food sustainable. Growing of food in cities is another important biophilic urban design strategy, as it offers the chance for urbanites to connect with soil and plants, to be outside, and to eat and savor healthful, tasty food. Rooftops and balconies around the city also offer the possibility of growing food, as well as injecting an element of greenness and nature, and increasingly many urban residents are doing just this. One city where vegetables can be seen growing on many rooftops and balconies is Montreal, Quebec. There, a nonprofit group called Alternatives runs the Montreal Rooftop Gardens Project, which started rooftop gardens in many buildings around the city. Their motto is "liberating new spaces for healthy cities." These urban gardens are lush and provide a dramatic green contrast to the stark grayness of buildings and tarmac. Like trees and ecological green walls and rooftops, these elevated vegetable gardens provide other green benefits, such as shading and cooling.

The vegetable gardens at McGill University in Montreal are some of the more impressive, and the food grown here supplies much of what is needed for a meals-on-wheels program for older residents. When I visited this garden, located on the roof of a university parking garage, it was producing an impressive amount of food in small, leftover spaces. Mostly in containers, the tentacles of string trellising were helping the pole beans and cucumbers shoot toward the sky and in many places creep up the walls and building façades.

The Montreal program is trying to get residents in that city to realize that food production is possible even where only a balcony is available. They have designed their own rooftop and balcony vegetable growing kit. It is essentially a recycling bin with a few other parts added, including a bendable platform at the bottom allowing for soil above and a water reservoir below. A watering pipe allows for easy watering and the occasional addition of organic fertilizer. Alternatives sells about five hundred of these kits each year. Each kit includes a manual with urban gardening tips, information on what sort of soil or growing material is needed, and when and how to fertilize the garden. Additional advice and guidance can be found on the project's Web site (www.rooftopgardens.ca/en).

Many of the in-between and leftover spaces in a city, even a very dense city, can be reprogrammed for food production. In the downtown Vancouver, B.C. neighborhood of Mole Hill, a dramatic example can be found of an alley converted from parking space to a beautiful, verdant oasis, designed by landscape architect Thomas Gould (of the firm Durante Kreuk, Ltd.). Car traffic is now restricted to a narrow, single, winding lane, flanked on both sides by lush, edible landscaping—raspberry and blackberry bushes—with car spaces converted to raised-bed gardens. There are places to sit and rest and even a section of a daylit stream to enjoy. There is still the occasional car passing through, but one is more likely to see residents strolling through on foot.

New urban development can and should now include places (rooftops, side yards, backyards) where residents can directly grow food. This has been a trend in Europe, as new urban ecological neighborhoods have included community gardens as a central design element (e.g., Viikki in Helsinki, and South False Creek in Vancouver). Integrating new development and food production is also happening in some innovative ways here in the United States.

But we can also reimagine our more suburban neighborhoods and living environments as opportunities to grow food. One of the more interesting recent examples of the idea of yard gardening can be found in a relatively new model, a business called Community Roots, that has taken root

Figure 4.4 Montreal rooftop garden. This photo shows an extensive food–producing garden on the roof of a parking garage at McGill University, in downtown Montreal. Photo credit: Tim Beatley

Figure 4.5 An alley in the downtown neighborhood of Mole Hill, in Vancouver. Photo credit: Tim Beatley

in south Boulder, Colorado. I had the chance to visit the project and hear firsthand from its brainchild, Kipp Nash, how the front yards and backyards in that city are being reimagined as spaces for growing food. Kipp has now assembled a collection of twelve yards in and around his neighborhood and is intensively cultivating these suburban spaces. The homeowner sometimes helps, but for the most part Kipp and his volunteers do the actual farming. In return, the homeowner gets to pick and eat some of the produce. Most of the production, however, is sold through Kipp's CSA and the Boulder farmers' market. The amount of food produced on these small spaces is impressive indeed, and he gets multiple harvests per bed. On the day I visited Kipp he showed me the leaf lettuce, spinach, salad turnips, and a visually dramatic forest of kale he was growing in his neighbor's yard.

The potential fruit production on a single urban or suburban lot is tremendous, and the new victory garden is capable of producing much more than most imagine. This is dramatically demonstrated by Greg Peterson, who operates what he calls the Urban Farm on a one-third-acre lot in a central Phoenix neighborhood. Greg has now planted more than seventy fruit trees on the urban farm and also uses the site for fruit tree classes, fruit tree sales and distribution, and a host of other urban agricultural endeavors (he raises chickens and vegetables on the site as well). He is able to fit so many trees because he plants smaller varieties and creatively uses the edges of the lot (planting fruit trees becomes a point of conversation and friendship building with his adjoining neighbors). In Charlottesville, at least one family has installed a front-yard vineyard, complete with professional trellising and an irrigation system. It's a distinctive look for a yard, but they are producing a great deal of grapes (and wine), zinfandel and pinot noir. The owners, the Stafford family, joke about the possibilities of their street, Dairy Road, becoming its own wine-growing region.[32]

Biophilic Urban Neighborhoods

Many of the opportunities to re-earth urban areas come together in new ways of thinking about the design and functioning of urban neighborhoods. There are often tremendous opportunities to retrofit existing urban neighborhoods, to better incorporate nature and natural features, as well as to design new neighborhoods with direct access to nature as a central design element. As Girling and Kellett argue, the neighborhood "represents a typical increment of urban development, a common but significant building block of contemporary cities, which is situated at a fascinating interaction

---

Box 4.2
Some Key Attributes of a Biophilic Neighborhood

— Connected streets and pathways throughout
— Abundant green areas to explore, play in, and gather in
— One or more nature trails nearby; a neighborhood meandering pathway connecting major destinations in the neighborhood
— Ability to move by foot or bicycle from doorstep or building stoop to regional nature
— Water: A remnant creek or stream or water body to visit
— Abundant nature throughout: Sidewalk gardens, yard farms, backyard woodlots
— Edible trees and bushes
— Designated neighborhood camping area
— One or more tree houses
— A neighborhood nature center
— Neighborhood nature docents: Neighborhood experts on a range of natural and biophilic topics give frequent talks and hikes
— Nature equipment lending libraries (stocked with such things as field guides, aquatic testing kits, portable microscopes, binoculars, and bat detectors)

of issues, scales and expertise."[33] See box 4.2 for some key attributes of a biophilic neighborhood.

New neighborhoods can be configured to better fit around and protect natural features, such as streams, woodlands, and other areas rich in biodiversity. They can be designed to facilitate pedestrian access to natural areas and a greater outdoor-oriented lifestyle. Existing neighborhoods can be retrofitted through many of the urban greening techniques already mentioned, including the daylighting of streams, the replacement of parking and hard surfaces with trees, vegetation, and permeable surfaces, and the conversion of turfgrass lawns into native prairies, for instance, and edible landscaping and gardens. We have an increasing number of good examples of these kinds of green urban neighborhoods from North America and Europe.[34] The challenge of creating more urban green neighborhoods is partly about urban design—the physical conditions and qualities of urban neighborhoods—and partly about the program of activities, relationships, and new roles that urbanites must assume in a biophilic neighborhood.

Two recent examples include the Greenwich Millennium Village in London and the Western Harbor in Malmö, Sweden—both brownfield redevelopment projects. In Greenwich Millennium Village there is a distinctive and creative combination of high-density sustainable housing and an impressive degree of access to nature. Residents have visual and pedestrian access to a restored riparian wetland system through a series of elevated boardwalks, bird blinds, and a nature center and viewing structure. Residents here are routinely watching nesting birds and aquatic life, often from their balconies, and experiencing daily what much of the Thames River ecosystem looked like prior to industrial development.

The Western Harbor in Malmö is a new urban district that provides 100 percent of the district's energy from local renewable sources. Including nature in this urban district was a key priority from the beginning, and builders have been subject to both a minimum greenspace factor (a formula stipulating minimum levels of greenery; more on that in chapter 5) and a system of green points. In the latter case, builders commit to achieving at least 10 green points out of a list of 35 green measures. Points were given for everything from installing nesting boxes or bat boxes, to establishing butterfly courtyards, to planting fruit trees, to installing a green rooftop. Although there is a considerable amount of hardscape here, the overall results are impressive. Green courtyards, native vegetation, and a meandering vegetated water channel snake through the neighborhood, creating natural sights and sounds that form the connective tissue of the neighborhood. The water sounds are never far away, adding much to the biophilic atmosphere.

The Western Harbor has an unusual street layout, an off-kilter grid, with most internal walkways off limits to cars. One of the city's project architects describes the neighborhood layout as being a bit like a maze and fostering, in her words "the enjoyment of being lost."[35] She is right, of course, and as we wandered together through the neighborhood, there was indeed a sense of exploration, a sense of discovery, and the pleasure of eventually popping out at the edge of the sea, with the bridge to Denmark in the background.

Other new dense urban neighborhoods in European cities offer a similar combination of nature and green design and density. Hammarby Sjöstad, a new ecological neighborhood in Stockholm, was designed with nature very close by for most residents, in a highly connected, walkable environment. Even more admirably, two green eco-ducts connect the neighborhood with a larger forested park, providing in this case safe passage to a large, mysterious, nature-ful world beyond the boundaries of one's block or neighborhood. In building this new neighborhood special attention was paid to protecting the stock of old oak trees, many now standing in close proximity to dense housing. A creatively designed footbridge leads residents to a grove of ancient oaks and a natural play area frequently visited by neighborhood kids.

Limiting Cars, Expanding Nature

These green neighborhoods have in common an urban form and design that minimizes the impact of cars and creates safe spaces for walking and other outdoor activity. Connected streets with sidewalks, car-free or car-limited neighborhood spaces, and trails that connect the neighborhood to larger networks of greenspace and nature are all important qualities. The car-limited neighborhood Vauban, in Freiburg, Germany, for instance, discourages car ownership (cars are permitted, but only in peripheral parking garages and at a significant cost to the resident), and the life of the neighborhood occurs around beautiful courtyard spaces where cars are not permitted and where kids play. These close-by neighborhood spaces in turn connect to larger green features (a nearby stream and a bridge connecting to a regional network of natural areas).[36]

Car-limited housing areas have been a trend in European cities, where it is perhaps easier because of the more compact urban form and abundance of alternatives to driving, including good public transit. In Vauban, the design of the residential areas is such that occasional car access

Figures 4.6, 4.7, and 4.8: Hammarby Sjöstad: ecobridge crossing highway, foot bridge to ancient oak grove, and forested trails beyond major highway. Photo credit: Tim Beatley

Figure 4.7

Figure 4.8

(for dropping off and picking up) is possible, but much of the neigh-borhood is comprised of a series of interior green courtyards that are not accessible by car. These are child and family play areas, real oases where parents do not have to worry about the dangers of errant drivers or flinch at the sound of a racing motor. Residents can own cars, but the financial ·incentives work against this: Residents must purchase a space in a peripheral parking lot, at a price of more than $20,000.[37] From the beginning, then, residents are encouraged to find other ways of getting around, which are quite abundant, including walking, bicycling, and a fast tram that runs through the neighborhood. Children and adults alike are well connected to the rest of the city, by the way.

Vauban, like many of the examples I have been discussing, scores high on the connectedness index: The neighborhood is highly permeable from a pedestrian and bicyclist point of view. One can move from the inte-rior green courtyard to other courtyards and greenspaces, and then reach a natural flowing creek at the edge of the neighborhood and proceed from there to larger and more distant parks and greenspaces. And the homes themselves are swathed in green, with creative trellising and plants creeping up the walls and stairwells of many of the attached housing units in the neighborhood.

In Understenshöjden, an eco-village in Stockholm, clustering has allowed for a remarkably small development footprint (the homes have been

designed and built to look as though they have been dropped in by heli-
copter) and the preservation of a marvelous forested environment, again
near transit and the center of the city. The eco-village also includes a host
of green building features, including solar water heating, use of nontoxic
paints, and other sustainable materials. Interspersed between the buildings
are small patios, tables, and outdoor eating areas where families informally
gather. Unpaved paths meander through the woods, connecting the homes
to each other and to a peripheral common parking area. The dominant
feeling of this place is of living (compactly) in a native forest, though in a
very urban setting. And in the forest near the homes is a rather large community tree house, which is undoubtedly a popular destination for the free-
ranging neighborhood kids.

Some emerging examples of sustainable urban developments that
more effectively connect with and embrace the nature and natural systems can be found in Noisette, a major sustainable redevelopment in North
Charleston, South Carolina, incorporating a portion of the former Charleston Naval Base. Ecological restoration and efforts to connect this emerging
sustainable district to the nature and hydrology of the site appear to be a
major part of the Noisette development concept, and a separate Noisette
preserve plan has been prepared. Restoration of Noisette Creek, which runs
through the project site and drains into the Cooper River, is a centerpiece
of the project (about 135 acres in size overall). The plan identifies a critical
buffer and new stormwater management features (bioswales), an interpre-
tive nature center, walking and biking trails, and a native plant nursery. The
plan also envisions undertaking a number of restoration measures, including
the planting of native tree species and the removal of fill and the reestablish-
ment of wetlands in certain areas.

The Noisette plan also identifies how, through a network of trails
and pathways, the creek will connect to surrounding neighborhoods. The
creek is also viewed as a significant educational resource for the fourteen schools that are located within two miles. The Michaux Conservancy
and Land Trust has been formed to manage and steward over the preserve
(and exists as a program within the Noisette Foundation).[38] The goal of the
Noisette Creek and the Michaux Conservancy is "reconnecting the local
population with nature" and serving as an outdoor classroom and research
laboratory.[39]

It is an interesting exercise to imagine how existing urban and
suburban neighborhoods might be reconfigured and redesigned to better
nurture connections with nature. Suburban lawns might be dug up and re-
planted with native plants and wildflowers, for instance, features that accommodate wildlife and wildness. One place where this idea is finding support

is Austin, Texas, where the city's former airport is being redeveloped into a biophilic neighborhood called Mueller (after the airport). This new green neighborhood will be flanked by a greenway, and the southwest portion of this will be restored as native blackland prairie, a collaborative project between RVi Planning and Landscape Architecture and the Ladybird Wildflower Center at the University of Texas. Only about 1 percent of blackland prairie habitat remains, and currently the closest place to find it is a two-hour drive from Austin. This restoration project has the possibility of not only restoring habitat but retaining stormwater, sequestering carbon, and, perhaps most important in this case, connecting future residents to the landscape history and ecology of this part of Texas. Discussions are now under way about how the residential areas of Mueller might further be populated with native flora, by encouraging (or perhaps mandating) that traditional turfgrass lawns be replaced, or partially replaced, with native grasses and flowers.

Re-Earthing Older Urban Neighborhoods

In many American cities, such as Cleveland and Detroit, there will be abundant opportunities to use and reconfigure abandoned lots to help restore and insert new forms of nature into existing urban neighborhoods. One or more lots might be assembled into new neighborhood gardens or community forests, for instance. In Cleveland, there are some 15,000 vacant lots and 3,300 acres of vacant land dispersed over the city, representing a tremendous opportunity to restore nature in urban neighborhoods close to where people live.

A project called Re-Imagining Cleveland explores a number of possibilities for reusing such lots as a way of restoring the city's ecology, generating new jobs, and helping to stabilize neighborhoods in decline. *Re-Imagining a More Sustainable Cleveland*, a report prepared by the Cleveland Urban Design Collaborative at Kent State University, was adopted by the city's Planning Commission in 2008.[40] The report concludes that these current land use and economic conditions "create unprecedented opportunities to improve the city's green space network and natural systems" and that Cleveland can "reinvent itself as a more productive, sustainable, and ecologically sound city."[41] The possibilities include putting some land aside for later development but transitioning much of this land into more productive uses, especially for ecosystem restoration and retention, urban agriculture, and renewable energy production (including the intriguing possibility of neighborhood-scale geothermal plants). The report sets out the ambitious target that every resident should be within a half mile (ideally a quarter mile, it states) of a community garden. There are spectacular challenges in transitioning to this green urban reuse, but if Cleveland can succeed, it might well be the model for how to balance urban renewal and pockets of urban density surrounded by highly green and desirable natural neighborhoods, where free-ranging kids can be found among the productive woodlots, riparian areas, and urban farms (of the food and energy kind). Liabilities are transformed into the backbone of a resilient and sustainable network of urban neighborhoods, and a model is created for the rest of the nation.

An impressive *Vacant Land Re-Use Pattern Book* has been prepared to stimulate thinking about how lots might be productively reconfigured.[42] Also prepared by Kent State, it works through a variety of reuse options, including opportunities for splitting lots between adjacent property owners, and ways to design in pocket parks and native plantings, new central market gardens by assembling multiple parcels, new rain gardens, and bioretention. I especially like the notion of central green natural parks. While the pattern book is just a beginning point, it helps one to visualize the ecological and community value of planting native forests in the city. Working urban landscapes could eventually be the source of sustainably harvested lumber and wood products or fruit, in the case of orchards.

One of the early projects in Cleveland exploring how existing neighborhoods could be greened is the Cleveland EcoVillage. Still evolving and developing, it represents an interesting model that envisions the layering of green and sustainable ideas and technologies onto an existing neighborhood in a struggling older community, in this case the Detroit-Shoreway neighborhood. Already much has been done, including constructing new green townhomes and green cottages, planting community gardens, and even integrating renewable energy production. At the center of the eco-village is the 65th Avenue station of the Regional Transit Authority (RTA), a heavy rail line that provides the neighborhood with quick and frequent service to downtown and to the airport in the opposite direction. As part of moving forward on the ecovillage, the RTA was convinced to build a new green station structure, providing the basis for a car-free, transit-oriented neighborhood (quite a shift, as the transit agency was close to shutting down the station and stop). Indeed, the ecovillage itself is defined in terms of the walking radius around this station.

Another key piece in the Cleveland EcoVillage is the ecological redevelopment and restoration of a 22-acre community recreation center and park, lying on the edge of the neighborhood. Now largely an empty turfgrass field, the neighborhood has developed, through a series of design charrettes, an impressive alternative vision. The vision includes needed ball fields and the more conventional recreational elements, including a series of trails through a new park, but it is more bold and more biophilic; it will also be a stormwater collection facility, it will prominently include fruit trees and edible landscaping, and much of the site will be returned to natural habitat and native plants.

While designing and building biophilic neighborhoods within existing cities on infill and recycled urban land, as in the case of the Cleveland EcoVillage, is preferable, there are many noteworthy efforts under way in more suburban, even exurban, locations. One interesting example is Harmony, Florida, a new community located south of Orlando, explicitly designed and managed to facilitate connection with nature and to foster awareness of animals and natural life. Still in the early stages of development, with about 300 units, at build-out the community will be home to about 18,000 residents. The majority of the acreage—about 70 percent of the site's 11,000 acres—will be left undeveloped. Much of the nature will be accessible through a trail system, including the use of an existing natural gas easement as a corridor linking different parts of the property. There are several beautiful and serene lakes, where noisy motorboats are forbidden and where many birds can be watched, including a number of sandhill cranes (*Grus canadensis*), which I viewed on a recent February visit.

Harmony seeks to foster a different kind of relationship to the environment for residents, and this starts from beginning. Those who buy new homes are generally given a briefing and tour at the Harmony Welcome Center. The packet of materials new residents receive includes lots of information about the unique natural environment. The town's conservation director, Greg Golgowski, feels the most difficult group to reach may be the second or third owner of a house. Real estate agents are encouraged to bring prospective buyers to the visitor's center but seldom do. One creative approach used in the past has been to provide financial incentives—awarding Harmony bucks that can be redeemed at the development's restaurant for agents and brokers who bring clients to the center, with an even larger redeemable amount in the event a homeowner actually buys.

Residents of Harmony enjoy a number of pathways to learning more about and connecting with this impressive environment. There is a conservation club to join, for example, with monthly meetings, and a youth farm. The town organizes an annual dark-sky festival, and such events represent other ways to connect. The event is a grand occasion, drawing some 2,500 people, mostly from outside Harmony. Preserving the spectacular views of the night sky has been a priority in Harmony. Dark sky-compliant street lighting is used throughout the community. Informative signage about native flora and fauna can be found in many of the parks and public spaces in Harmony. There are seven main panels and twenty-eight different educational storyboards that are rotated, all developed by students and faculty at the University of Florida.

Biophilic and Healthy Buildings

Regions and cities and urban neighborhoods are essential biophilic units, but much of daily life and work occurs in buildings and homes, which can also be biophilic. Hospitals, schools, offices, and of course homes and apartments can through careful and conscious design create the conditions for happier, healthier, and more productive lives. Two summers ago I had the pleasure of touring a remarkable building that convinced me of the power of biophilic design. The newly opened Dell Children's Medical Center in Austin, Texas provides inspiration and insight about what biophilic buildings might look and feel like. This 430,000-square-foot building, with 195 beds, is an unusual hospital in its core emphasis on biophilic design qualities. And they are many: Natural daylight floods into virtually all of the spaces of this building (no room or space is more than thirty-two feet from a window, with the exception of the surgery department), and there are five interior open-air courtyards in the building and two healing gardens. The courtyards provide light and opportunities for outside activity and access to nature. The courtyards and gardens contain plants and landscaping native to one of the seven primary ecosystems in the 46-county service area of the hospital. One central courtyard even contains a multilevel waterfall, integrating the sights and sounds of water into the daily regime of this healing facility. Spending time in this building, awash in natural daylight, I found it easy to believe the environmental psychologist's groundbreaking work concluding that hospital patients in rooms with views of nature recover more quickly.[43]

The hospital has a number of other green features, including the recycling of building materials (including some 46,000 tons of asphalt), water-conserving bathroom fixtures, rainwater collection and reuse, low-VOC paints, and use of local building materials. Notably, the hospital includes local stone, specifically West Texas sandstone and Leuders limestone, adding another biophilic dimension.

Dell Children's Medical Center is also part of a larger biophilic community, the green redevelopment of the city's former Mueller airport

Figure 4.9 Dell Children's Hospital, Austin, Texas. Photo credit: Tim Beatley

(discussed above). When completed over the next decade, the new neighborhood will be highly walkable and also green, with an extensive greenspace network and re-created prairie ecosystem. The only evidence of
the airport will be the distinctive (for a residential neighborhood) old control tower and also a few hangar buildings that have been renovated and
reused.

Green features in office buildings and work environments can result not only in dramatic improvements in working conditions but also in
significant increases in productivity, carrying a substantial economic gain.[44]
One example is the new Council House 2, the municipal offices for the
City of Melbourne, Australia. This building incorporates a number of creative and higher-tech green design elements (wind turbines at the top of
the structure that pull air through the building, shower towers that provide evaporative cooling, and a wastewater harvesting system, among others), but perhaps most impressive are the basic biophilic and healthy features
of the structure—fresh outside air (no recirculated air) and lots of daylight
and plants. These green and healthy conditions were expected to result in
a 5 percent increase in worker productivity (with an economic value that
would pay for the cost of the green features in about ten years). A 2008
study showed that following the first full year of occupancy of the building,
worker productivity actually increased 10 percent, and the payback period is
only five years or less.[45]

Daylit and healthy buildings can help to stimulate healthy behaviors. A green building in Sydney, 30 The Bond, has both elevators and stairwells for moving up and down. The stairwells were designed to provide a
beautiful view of this very open-layout structure, with almost panoramic
and multifloor views of its large atrium and open areas, including a very
interesting heritage feature in the form of a bare (and dripping) granite wall
originally mined by convicts. Elevator use is about half of what it was expected to be because so many of the building's workers actively seek out
the stairwells.

There are many other examples of buildings that bring the outdoors in, that creatively incorporate green and natural elements, that design
with fresh air and daylight as essential elements. Much design thinking in
recent years has focused on the greening of larger high-rise structures and
the incorporation of, for instance, sky gardens, in larger office structures,
such as the Commerzbank building in Frankfurt, Germany, designed by
Norman Foster architects. Ken Yeang has designed some very notable biophilic high-rise structures that incorporate gardens, both interior and exterior. Some of the more ambitious ideas for integrating green elements
and greenspaces into high-density urban structures may seem whimsical or

unrealistic today but may be essential approaches of larger urban greening strategies in our increasingly urbanized world.

One especially interesting structure designed and built for the Hanover world's fair demonstrated this potential vision. The Dutch Pavilion was designed by the innovative Rotterdam firm of MVRVD and included an entire open floor of the structure as forest park—it was essentially a forest in the air, demonstrating the compelling theme of "Holland creates space." In fact the building was designed to show how different ecosystems of the Netherlands could be stacked or layered vertically, with a series of specially designed wind turbines on the top layer. While the notion of an open-air, mid-altitude urban park is a bit foreign to us today, it is perhaps not that different from buildings with rooftop parks and gardens or midlevel terraces where trees and greenery and access to fresh air and sunlight are available.

Several new high-rise structures in New York City highlight biophilic design features, including the 55-story Bank of America Tower: "Higher ceilings and extremely transparent low iron, low-e insulating glass in floor-to-ceiling windows permit maximum daylight in interior spaces, optimal views and energy efficiency."[46] The structure sits close to Bryant Park (the building's south end faces the park), and one of my favorite biophilic features of the building is its emphasis on pedestrian mobility. It is not far from a subway station, and no parking spaces are included in the plans for the building.

Renovations of existing structures, one of the most sustainable forms of green building in part because of the savings in materials and embodied energy, can also advance biophilic urbanism. Restoring and adaptively reusing existing structures not only has clear green advantages (embodied energy) but also often involves conserving textures and building materials that may be biophilic in nature and connect us to the past. Some older retrofits are also able to incorporate contemporary biophilic design elements. The Jean Vollum Natural Capital Center in Portland, Oregon, for instance, is an adaptive reuse of a former warehouse but with many newer green elements, such as green rooftops, stormwater retention bioswales, bicycle racks, and a parking lot that is frequently converted to a farmers' market. There are also some novel elements, including (my favorite) public drinking fountains with an image of Mt. Hood attached, meant to instill sensitivity about where water derives from. There is an impressive outdoor terrace, with chairs and a fireplace, that encourages workers to connect visually and physically with the outside.[47]

Single-family homes can also be designed in ways that facilitate more contact with nature. Designing with passive solar in mind, to allow breezes and natural ventilation, and with native vegetation and habitat rather than traditional lawns would help to reconnect residents to the natural world. There are also increasingly creative ways to blur the lines between indoors and outdoors in home design.

Some homes have been designed to incorporate a stargazing tower and other biophilic features. Might we imagine built-in places for microscopes or insect collecting, or nature stations, in the same way we now think of computer and television rooms?

Mike Archer and Bob Beale have written *Going Native*, a book suggesting a host of provocative yet creative ways to reconnect Australians to their incredible native biodiversity. Perhaps the most intriguing idea, and a charge to architects, is to design homes that treat urban wildlife as an opportunity to learn about and reconnect with nature rather than as a nuisance:[48]

> People often complain about opossums (*Didelphis virginiana*) in the roof doing unseen "things," yet at the same time they complain about their square-eyed children spending hours in front of the television watching junk. Why not construct houses so that they actively accommodate native animals such as possums, bats, and native bees? Imagine a house—as suggested by biologist Nick Mooney—constructed with a central well from ceiling to floor that had large one-way glass windows enclosing a space with artistically distributed vegetation (nourished by skylights in the roof and soft lights at night) as well as logs. In this in-house refuge, possums could make nests, mate, raise babies, feed, feud, and provide hours of fascinating evening viewing for the human family. Even watching parrots feed in native trees outside a large picture window is a visual and aural treat to start off the working day.

The irony is that in many places in the United States expelling wildlife from homes and attics is a major headache and stressful aspect of homeownership. There is little thought put into how wildlife might actually be invited in with new home designs that help to deflect and solve these problems.

Wherever possible we should design buildings—homes, offices, and institutional structures—that nudge us to leave the confines of interior space. An example close to home for me is the green addition to Campbell Hall, the School of Architecture building at the University of Virginia. The southern side of the building has been designed to form a sheltered outdoor classroom space, which has become very popular, with movable chairs and an outdoor chalkboard. It sits at the beginning of a green bioswale system that collects and celebrates rainwater. Whenever possible, institutional and office buildings should be designed to provide outdoor eating, strolling, and gathering spaces suitable for meetings or conferences. Using creative windbreaks and even occasional use of outdoor heaters, we might entice urbanites to spend more of their productive day in the outside world.

Greening the Vertical: Green Walls and Green Rooftops

In applying a biophilic urban design in dense urban environments it becomes essential to see the many leftover spaces as opportunities for green, for nature creep in and occupy and grow into the urban fabric. In dense cities there will always be many surfaced spaces where this can happen, but there will also have to be greening and growing in the more vertical and elevated environments. These spaces include rooftops and building façades, balconies and window openings, terraces and fire escapes, among many others.

Few urban greening ideas have picked up as much speed as quickly as green rooftops. With a long history of use in European cities, the last decade has seen remarkable progress in mainstreaming this idea in North American cities. A common distinction is made between extensive green rooftops (which usually cover an entire rooftop, with a relatively shallow substrate of soil and plants), and intensive green rooftops (larger trees and vegetation, usually covering only a small portion of roof or balcony). And while both forms can be important biophilic strategies, it is the extensive form that has taken off in recent years.

The many benefits of green rooftops are remarkable and explain their growing appeal: among other things, they help to cool buildings, resulting in significant energy savings; they effectively retain stormwater (often 75% of the rainwater falling on the roof is retained there, a key motivation for using them in American cities with high amounts of impervious surface and combined sewer overflow problems); and they sequester carbon, create new habitat, and result in much more natural, biophilic views and spaces for urbanites. And, while there can be an increased upfront cost, green rooftops dramatically extend the life of the underlying roof, more than paying for the expense of installation.[49]

A Toronto-based nonprofit called Green Roofs for Healthy Cities has been active in promoting and educating about green roofs throughout North America. They offer training and certification for green roof professionals and host an annual green roof conference.[50]

Few U.S. cities have seen as much progress in green roofs as Chicago, which in many ways has been the epicenter of activity. Under the

Figure 4.10 Native species of cactus on the green rooftop of the César Pelli–designed Minneapolis Public Library. Photo credit: Tim Beatley

leadership of Mayor Richard Daley, city hall has been famously retrofitted with a green roof, and through example and financial incentives there are now some 450 green rooftops in Chicago.

Green rooftops are now becoming mainstream practice in the United States, and there are few cities lacking in good examples. In Minneapolis, the city's new César Pelli–designed library has a green rooftop that contains, among other species, native cacti.

The new Ballard branch of the Seattle Public Library shows how building-integrated green features can be an asset to the surrounding neighborhood. While the building incorporates a number of ecological features, including extensive use of skylights, daylighting, recycled materials, and photovoltaics, its most prominent feature is its extensive green rooftop. The dramatic sloping roof is home to more than eighteen thousand native plants. The roof is a mix of some fourteen different native grass species, including woolly yarrow, long-stoloned sedge, red creeping fescue, and fool's onion. These grass species give the roof the look of a native prairie, visible from all of the sidewalks and spaces around the building.

Rooftops provide yet another opportunity for new parks where space is limited in the city. In Freiburg, Germany, in the Resielfeld neigh-

Figure 4.11 Rooftop of the Ballard branch of the Seattle Public Library. Photo credit: Tim Beatley

borhood, there was a need for a new community sports hall but no place to put it that would not result in a diminution of park space. The answer was an unusual design for the structure, essentially with a round green rooftop covering a sports hall below. The result is a pedestrian connection allowing one to walk on and across the roof of the structure and a park that has an unusual look and feel.

Experience has shown that over time substantial biodiversity can take hold on green rooftops, and in some cities ecological roofs can even help in reestablishing populations of endangered and threatened species. Green roofs can be designed to maximize the native biodiversity they support through methods such as using soil and substrate materials from the region and varying the thickness of the substrate and soil. As Swiss green roof researcher Stephan Brenneisen concludes, "Designing green roofs so that they have varying substrate depths and drainage regimes creates a mosaic of microhabitats on and below the soil surface and can facilitate colonization by a more diverse flora and fauna."[51] We should design green rooftops in our cities as opportunities to see and celebrate the natural plant assemblages that existed in an urban bioregion.

It is perhaps different, albeit useful, to understand green rooftops in the city as potential biological reservoirs, as places where struggling species might be reestablished, as nurseries from which native species of plants and invertebrates might be propagated. And these rooftops will also offer fantastic opportunities to research and monitor what local species do well and where volunteers might be enlisted to botanically and biologically colonize other barren spaces in the city.

But of course we need to think beyond rooftops and imagine other possibilities. One interesting idea is to profoundly rethink the many vertical spaces in cities, which could, like green rooftops, help to infuse nature as well as sequester carbon, reduce energy consumption, retain stormwater, and help to tackle the urban heat island phenomenon. Patrick Blanc is one of the most creative designers of organic or green walls, in both interior and exterior spaces. He is a botanist by profession (employed at the French National Center for Scientific Research), and his vertical gardens, or *murs vegetals* (plant walls) as he prefers, are beautiful and lush and add an incredible degree of greenness to urban buildings. Created by a metal exterior frame, with plastic and felt layers through which the plants are rooted, garden walls like the visually dramatic one he designed for the Musée du Quai Branly in Paris is kind of vertical hydroponics. Many of the plants used (some 170 different species) have been discovered and carried back from botanic expeditions in many parts of the world, and each project uses a different botanic mix, depending on site and climate conditions.

I recently traveled to Paris to see and film several of Patrick Blanc's most notable green walls. I had seen many photos of his wall at the Musée du Quai Branly, and while the photos are impressive, they do not prepare you for the real thing. In fact there were two aspects of the wall that I had not expected. The first was the texture and structure of the green wall. While it is a vertical wall, it is remarkably horizontal. There are rather large bushes and various other green vegetation extending outward from the wall several feet. The marvelously nonvertical structure means it provides quite a bit of shade for the street below. The green plantings, moreover, extend down to the ground, and so this structure allows touching and eye-to-eye interaction (some of the other green walls that Blanc has designed are higher up on the building, where this direct personal experience becomes more difficult, where the wall essentially becomes a visual experience, albeit a delightful one).

The second remarkable thing about this wall is just how magical its effect on passersby seems to be. The wall faces a sidewalk that serves as a major pedestrian corridor for tourists (the Eiffel Tower is a mere block or so away). It is seemingly impossible for pedestrians to walk by the wall without

Figure 4.12 One of botanist Patrick Blanc's most famous green walls, Paris. Photo credit: Tim Beatley

interacting with it in some way. They stop to touch it, to gaze up at it, and to stand loved ones and family members in front of it to take photos. The reaction is something akin to viewing the wall as a kind of natural wonder, and the picture taking is similar to what might happen in front of Niagara Falls. Part of this must surely be the factor of surprise. The wall is not expected, and for most it would be an unusual sight anywhere.

Spectacular Blanc walls are also appearing in other cities. One of the most visually striking is the vertical garden at the CaixaForum Museum in Madrid. It frames one side of a large public square. Green and wooly, it boasts some 15,000 plants and 250 different species on a 24-meter-high wall. Perhaps Blanc's most ambitious project to date is London's Athenaeum Hotel, where he has designed a dramatic eight-story green wall. Containing some 12,000 plants and 260 different plant species, the wall wraps completely around one corner of the hotel structure, leading one journalist to refer to it as an "antigravity forest."[52]

Blanc has said he "likes to reintegrate nature where one least expects it": in a metro station, in a hotel lobby, on the side of a department store building. These, he feels, are essentially the remaining spaces available to the city. "Humanity is living more and more in cities, and at odds with

Figure 4.13
Another of Blanc's
new green wall
designs, this one
in Madrid, Spain.
Photo credit:
Tim Beatley

nature. . . . The plant wall has a real future for the well-being of people living in cities. The horizontal is finished—it's for us. But the vertical is still free."[53]

Green walls of various kinds are popping up in many cities around the world. There are now hundreds in Canada and Australia. Mark Paul, of the Green Wall Company in Sydney, Australia, for instance, has designed and installed green walls in many places, including the Quantas first-class lounge at the Sydney international airport (using epiphyte plants). A dramatic Canadian example can be found at the University of Guelph–Humber campus in Toronto. Here, a wall designed by Air Quality Solutions Ltd. impressively occupies the main interior atrium of the building, providing a striking living feature and green backdrop for students and workers and at the same time cleansing the air.[54]

One of the more dramatic examples of the use of green walls in a city can be seen in the work of Korean architect Minsuk Cho and his firm Mass Studies. Specifically, he has designed a dramatic green building for the Seoul store of Belgian fashion designer Ann Demeulemeester. The shop is essentially covered in blankets of *Pachysandra terminalis*, a common ground-cover, from street surface to roof. There is also an interior stairwell dramatically covered with moss, and bamboo is used for exterior landscaping.

Not only are green walls becoming more mainstream, but designers and city leaders are envisioning even bolder ways to insert them into cities. Recently plans for retrofitting an eighteen-story high-rise building in Portland, Oregon included one of the largest green walls anywhere. The wall will consist of a series of trellises that would extend some 250 feet to cover much of the west side of the building. The Edith Green–Wendell Wyatt Federal Building would sport a most visually dramatic green element—essentially a series of seven "vegetated fins" extending along the façade. As the visual and ecological value of green walls becomes clearer over time, we will likely see more applications on this scale.

Many other green elements can be and have been integrated into building design and site, including green courtyards, skygardens and green atria, and rooftop and vertical food production systems.

Biophilic Schools

A biophilic city is one that understands the tremendous potential to move society in the direction of deeper connection with the natural world by reforming both the physical circumstances and curriculum and pedagogy of its public schools. And there are many positive reasons to support green and biophilic schools, including impressive improvements in the test scores of students.[55]

Some of the most compelling examples of biophilic schools can be found in Australian cities. Few schools are doing as much as the Noranda Primary School, which I greatly enjoyed visiting. Located in the Bayswater Council, in northern Perth, this school has placed a priority on preserving a significant natural area, a beautiful bushland, on the school grounds and incorporating natural heritage and bushland conservation values into its curriculum. Remarkably intact, for the most part, though degraded in parts, the remnant forested bush is home to an abundant and diverse flora and fauna—grass, trees, red gums, even orchids, including at least one rare species. There are many school activities and classes that use the bush, and it is the site of daily walks by the students. It has taken the place of some of the more conventional forms of school equipment typically seen on school grounds. There is a Bush Wardens program, where participating students are involved in a variety of activities aimed at learning and caring more about this natural area. Students in all grades at Noranda, whether or not they are participating in the Bush Wardens program, are taught about the bush, and the school has commissioned a special curricular manual, *Our Bushland Classroom*, to help in this pedagogical mission. The surrounding residential neighborhood, moreover, is able to join in the enjoyment and appreciation of this impressive site of local nature.

There are also a number of impressive European examples of biophilic schools. One of these, another public green demonstration project in Copenhagen, is actually an ecological daycare. Built in 2002, the Stenurten ("stonecrop") center includes use of daylight, natural ventilation, and natural building materials. Its most dramatic feature is its sloping wall of glass that harvests sunlight but also facilitates natural ventilation of the structure. The students are also growing on-site some of the food they eat, learning about organic and local food even at this very early stage of life.

There are few schools as green and biophilic as the Sidwell Friends School in Washington, D.C. A new green middle school was added and the lower school underwent a green renovation, both designed by the architectural firm Kieran Timberlake. The main building has a passive solar design and includes extensive natural daylight. The architects describe the building as "a compass, revealing orientation through the configuration of exterior sunscreens. At the north no screening is needed, and north-facing windows fully admit diffuse light. At the south screening is most effective when placed horizontally above windows. At the east and west vertical sunscreens keep out glare when the sun is low."[56] The building also incorporates natural ventilation (use of solar chimneys), to bring air through the structure, a rooftop garden where students grow food, some photovoltaic panels that produce a portion of the electricity needed for the building, use of sustainable and largely local materials (nearly 80% of the building materials have been sourced within 500 miles of the site), and a constructed wetland system that treats wastewater from the building. The rainwater collection system is intended to educate about the local watershed. "A series of scuppers, open downspouts and gutters, flow forms and spillways direct rainwater to a biology pond which will support native habitat adjacent to the courtyard entry at the low point of the site, just as the Rock Creek watershed flows through the highlands down to the Potomac."[57] Some of the distinctive building materials that have been reused here include wood siding made from wine casks.

The Sidwell Friends example shows the importance and value of going well beyond the building itself, and there are many features of the curriculum and operation of the school that reflect biophilic values. There are AP environmental science classes and even an English class focused on environmental literature. There is ecological housekeeping and cleaning in the school, a green food service, and a school club called ECO (Environmentally Conscious Organization). Students are also encouraged to record their wildlife sightings and to post them on the school Web site.

How kids are transported to and from school is another key issue in the biophilic city. In the United States in just about forty years' time we have moved from half of school-aged kids walking or bicycling to school to fewer than 10 percent today.[58] There are many reasons, of course, including (again) fear by parents, the unsafe conditions of car-dependent communities, and the distances involved (the shift toward larger schools that essentially require driving). This trend toward driving contributes to the sedentary lifestyles and rising obesity levels in children. It also disconnects families from their community and nature. Every school should see the trip to and from a school as an opportunity to get children outside and active and get a sense of the outside wonder.

One idea, generally attributed to Australia street activist David Enwight, is the walking school bus (WSB). It is essentially an organized walk, supervised by parents, along a pre-set route. Parent volunteers escort the children to the school, then from the school back to their homes in the afternoon, much as a conventional school bus would. The results have been impressive, and in addition to getting kids outside and helping to slightly nudge them out of their sedentary patterns, there are other important social and learning benefits: "Particularly for new immigrants, this initiative creates community cohesion, provides an opportunity to socialize with other parents and develop a relationship with the school. The research also showed that having this relationship between home, community and school results in better outcomes for students—they tend to do better and as a result, stay in formal schooling longer."[59]

One of the largest WSB programs anywhere can be found in Auckland, New Zealand. Here there are some 260 different routes and some 4,700 students and 2,000 parents participating. The Auckland Regional Transport Authority supports the walking school buses through its demand management program (TravelWise) by providing start-up grants for new WSB routes and small annual operating funds.[60]

In my own city of Charlottesville, there are a remarkable number of schools within a short block or two of a park or greenspace, including an extensive twenty-mile-long trail system, yet students rarely visit these spaces before or after school or during the day. The school agenda in biophilic cities recognizes the value and importance of nearby nature and finds ways to steer and guide the young people in its charge to visit and enjoy them.

On a visit to Freiburg in 2008 we were able to film at a remarkable kindergarten. Thanks to the city's chief planner, Wulf Daseking, we were able to walk through the school, filming for *Nature in Cities*. The first thing you notice when you arrive at the front of the school is the very full rack of bicycles. Partly a function of the compact form of the neighborhood (and city), these children for the most part rode their bikes to school. Daseking explained, "It's the normal way, they just do it." When you walk into the structure, you are immediately awash in daylight streaming in from the large skylights traversing the center of the roof. Also striking is that the building is essentially a structure with few borders or enclosures. Perhaps this changes in winter, but there were no clear demarcations showing where inside ended and outside began. At the edge of the classrooms were a series of clever transitions, including fabric shades and sand boxes and play areas. The children were fully exploring the outside and clearly not constrained by any sense of being inside or being contained by the structure. Outside they are running in and out of interesting structures and garden areas, balancing on retaining walls, vigorously exploring, and playing with relatively little (apparent) supervision.

Concluding Thoughts

We don't lack tools and strategies for bringing nature back into cities, and there are an increasing number of compelling stories and examples of cities successfully doing just this. In some cases it is about looking for opportunities to let nature reestablish itself, while in others more aggressive urban interventions are required. The opportunities are many and both large and small: Entire watersheds and river systems that bisect larger urban areas, like the L.A. River, and many seemingly modest neighborhood greening projects can cumulatively add up to a significant amount of urban nature. In many cases we are already building new things in our cities—hospitals, parks, housing—so why not make them greener and integrate biophilic thinking and measures into the heart of their design? Increasingly, though, the agenda is about looking at less conventional places and ways of inserting and growing nature—rooftops, building façades, alleys, balconies, and sidewalks. Even vertical parks and forests, located in and on new high-rise structures in cities, are likely in our future.

Addressing larger sustainability issues often provides the space (figuratively and literally) to incorporate new nature. If we can reduce the impact of cars and car dependence, for instance, we have more room for trees, flowers, and urban wildlife. It is at once about creating not only the broader structure that encourages biophilic lives in cities—compactness and density and walkability—but also a host of more specific green interventions. It's about larger structure and patterns, with the many smaller steps that occur within those larger patterns.

Five

New Tools and Institutions to Foster Biophilic Cities

Moving cities in the direction of recognizing and fostering biophilic qualities will not be easy and will require significant and sustained investments in social and governmental infrastructure. Physical design, at the building, neighborhood, city, and regional levels, will only take us part of the way in creating a truly biophilic city. In addition to new design and planning codes and incentives that institutionalize biophilic design and planning, we need institutions that educate about nature or facilitate access and nudge us to explore nature and to live more outdoor lives.

Part of the challenge of achieving biophilic cities will be recognizing that there are many obstacles—some larger social and cultural, others legal, economic, and regulatory—embedded in obsolete planning systems. We need to fashion programs and policies and to develop new institutional capabilities and new forms of social capital that help to overcome these obstacles. What follows aims to sketch out the tools and larger institutions needed to shift toward biophilic cities. There is no example of a single city with everything in place, but there are many creative and inspiring examples of cities developing many of the necessary institutions and tools.

New Biophilic Design and Planning Standards

Plans and planning codes in American cities often fail to mandate, and may even discourage, the integration of nature in urban design. This is changing slowly, as more cities recognize the merits of green infrastructure. Some cities now have a greenway or open space minimum. Davis, California, for instance, requires that a minimum 15 percent of a site be set aside for greenways. And a number of cities, such as Chicago, now mandate minimum (and fairly extensive) landscaping requirements—for example, new shade trees must be planted (e.g., in Chicago, one shade tree for each 25 feet of road frontage).[1] These are good beginnings.

Some communities like Portland, Oregon have put into place a system of green density bonuses. Under Portland's eco-roof density bonus, developers can increase permissible density in exchange for the installation of a green rooftop, using a sliding scale (the greater the extent of the roof covered, the larger the bonus). Chicago and Seattle have adopted similar density bonuses, and Chicago even requires installation of green rooftops for buildings that receive financial assistance from the city.[2] Mandating the installation of green rooftops in flat-roof structures is common in cities in Germany and Switzerland.

In May 2009 Toronto became the first major North American city to adopt a mandatory green roof requirement. The Green Roof Bylaw mandates that all new residential and commercial rooftops over 2,000 m² of (gross) rooftop space must install a green roof, beginning in 2010 (and for industrial buildings, 2011).[3] The coverage required is graduated—the larger the roof, the larger the percentage of it that must be covered. Rooftops that are 5,000 m² or less must cover a minimum of 20 percent, while the percentage rises to 60 percent for rooftops of 20,000 m² or greater.

The city of Berlin has pioneered the concept of a Biotope Area Factor (BAF), an expression of the minimum proportion of a site in the city center that is required to contain green features or elements.[4] The Berlin idea has been applied in other European cities (e.g., Malmö, Sweden) and is often called a greenspace factor. Seattle, Washington has become the first American city to use this tool, calling it the Green Factor. The Seattle Green Factor is a requirement that new commercial development of 4,000 square feet or larger incorporate adequate green or landscape elements, usually expressed in terms of a percentage of the lot that must be greened. Development must reach a score of 0.30 (the equivalent of 30% of the lot), utilizing a "weighted menu of landscape elements."[5] Developers use a Green Factor worksheet that assigns a score for bioretention features (e.g., rain gardens), tree planting, green roofs and vegetated walls, water features, and permeable paving. Since January 2007, some sixty projects have already been evaluated in the program. Recent updates to the system provide bonuses for drought-tolerant or native plants, use of harvested rainwater, visible landscaping, and food cultivation.[6] One clear advantage of the Green Factor system is that it provides developers with a degree of flexibility in determining the specific mix of green features they wish to incorporate.

Establishing minimum biophilic city standards for all new neighborhoods and city projects is one possible strategy. Another possible strategy is the provision of incentives or upfront funding—grants and loans—to facilitate the installation of green features. Often green urban elements yield clear and demonstrable economic return to their owners—for instance, by reducing the cooling costs of a home or enhancing its sale price—even before broader public benefits and values are taken into account, but they are often avoided because of real or perceived additional upfront costs. This barrier is overcome in many European cities by generous government subsidies to support the installation of green rooftops.[7]

Chicago's green rooftop program offers installation grants, and in Portland the Metropolitan Services District ("Metro") has a Nature in Neighborhoods program that provides capital grants to support neighborhood greening projects.[8] "Nature in Neighborhoods is a broad-based regional initiative to restore and protect the region's natural assets."[9] Begun in 2005, the initiative provides funding both for restoration and enhancement grants and for capital grants. To date, Metro has awarded some $1.23 million in restoration grants to individuals and organizations in the region to support sixty-four projects. Through its matching grant requirement it has leveraged this to a total value of $4.6 million.[10]

Capital grants are intended to fund land acquisition and larger capital asset purchases, subject to a set of "key threshold criteria." Funding for these grant programs has been provided through a natural area bond measure (2006) and a Metro excise tax on solid waste. The Nature in Neighborhoods program also includes an effort to promote "nature friendly development" and has convened a series of workshops and seminars for area developers and a design competition that has further helped to generate ideas about how to integrate nature in greater Portland.

Demonstration projects and exhibits of various kinds can also encourage a move to greener projects. Paris, for instance, has installed a temporary biodiversity garden in front of the Place de l'Hôtel de Ville, the city hall. Called a "garden for a time," it both educates about biodiversity and plant life in the city and shows how it is possible to green very urban spaces. The retrofitting of Chicago's City Hall, at the behest of Mayor Daley, with a green rooftop had a significant impact in terms of advancing the notion of green rooftops in that city and, along with other green roof support programs, has ignited a strong interest in the installation of green rooftops (now 450 in that city either constructed or in the planning stages).

Various urban fee and taxing systems could be reformed to encourage or give preference to biophilic features. Municipal property tax systems, for instance, could factor in the presence or absence of trees and wildlife habitat, recognizing the high economic value that resources provide to the city (essentially subtract that value from a homeowner's tax bill). Stormwater and municipal utility bills could be structured, moreover, in ways that

Figure 5.1 The "Garden for a Time" installed in front of the Paris City Hall. Photo credit: Tim Beatley

encourage nature and natural features. For instance, it is common in German communities to assess water rates according to the extent of the permeable surface, giving a positive financial incentive to green rooftops and permeable spaces. A number of communities in the United States have formed or are forming stormwater management districts and putting into place a similar fee structure. The City of Greensboro, North Carolina, for instance, assesses a stormwater fee on both residential and commercial development, based on the extent of the impervious surface on a parcel.[11]

Cities might also underwrite programs and activities that entice residents to experience nature and to spend more time outside. Sometimes these subsidies or inducements are offered by nonprofits and NGOs working in a city. One notable nonprofit working in the Boston area is Community Boating, Inc. This volunteer-based not-for-profit 501(c)3 corporation dates back to 1936, when it was formed by Joseph Lee Jr., who saw a need to provide summer activities for kids on the west end of the city. Its stated mission is "the advancement of sailing for all by minimizing economic and physical obstacles to sailing."[12] The Junior program offers a season of sailing lessons (from June to August) for kids ten to eighteen years old for only $1. Setting kids down the course of an outdoor (in this case, boating and aquatic) life seems a tremendous gift, with many long-term social and health benefits, and well worth the subsidy. Some 2,500 kids participated in this program during the 2009 sailing season.[13] The nonprofit operates a fleet of more than seventy Cape Cod Mercury sailboats. Most recent has been a partnership between Community Boating, the city's parks and recreation department, and the Gensyme Corporation to operate a similar program for physically disabled residents, using specially modified sailboats.

There are other ways that localities and municipalities can help fill the funding voids. Neighborhood greening improvements, for instance, might be financed though the creative help of local governments through the use of taxing districts, something that is becoming extremely popular as a way to overcome the upfront costs associated with solar and renewable energy investments. Cities in California have led the way by creating taxing districts in which bonds can be floated to fund neighborhood improvements. The bonds are payable in increments over twenty years by a modest property tax increase.[14] A number of other states, including Ohio and Maryland, have followed suit. One can imagine any number of ambitious biophilic retrofits—perhaps installing a community forest or orchard, converting conventional streets to green infrastructure, installing green rooftops, perhaps even building new neighborhood nature centers—with this funding technique. As with municipal funding for solar installation, the biophilic improvements will likely enhance property values and provide economic value that exceeds the property tax liability.

Overcoming Regulatory Barriers

Even if individuals, families, and communities wish to green their environments, there are often regulatory barriers, some quite large, that get in the way. While sensitivity to the value of these regulations is necessary, there are often many ways in which street and engineering standards can be relaxed and made more flexible, providing new areas for growing nature and building community while also protecting human health and safety. In a number of cities there are new efforts to give neighborhood and community groups greater direct power and tools to green their neighborhoods. Through the work of the Ashoka Community Greens program, the City of Baltimore has now adopted the Alley Gating and Greening ordinance, which clearly lays out the steps and conditions under which residents are allowed to close or partially close alleys behind their homes (which have become dangerous, gray, and neglected areas) and create green community gathering spaces. To gate an alley requires approval from 100 percent of the property owners abutting the alley (only 80% for alley greening projects that don't impede vehicular travel), and a number of alleys are now accessible only through key locks. The Ashoka program has also produced a very useful "Alley Gating and Greening Toolkit" that walks residents through the permitting process and provides many tips and much information about how and in what ways an alley can be transformed.[15]

The results of the Community Greens initiatives are impressive, and the transformation of many of Baltimore's depressing alleys has been remarkable. The Ashoka Web site (www.ashoka.org) contains before and after photos that tell much of the story. The Luzerne/Glover alley in the Patterson Park neighborhood is typical. Before the gating and greening, it was a depressing and badly neglected space. The after photos show considerable improvements: benches and outside furniture, new trees and flowers in planters, a barbecue grill, and, most important, people socializing and kids playing in the space. Preliminary results suggest that greening alleys enhances the attractiveness of these neighborhoods, raises property values, and brings people together.[16]

In Portland, Oregon, through the advocacy of the community group City Repair, the city adopted an intersection repair ordinance, giving every neighborhood the right to take back and personalize the intersections closest to their homes as potential gathering and socializing spots. The results are spectacular in the colorfully painted intersections at Share-it-Square and Sunnyside Piazza. Here the paint designs have injected vivid colors, a sense that the spaces are public or community and that the neighborhood is actively caring for these spaces. Research suggests that compared with conventional intersections in other similar neighborhoods in Portland, these unique neighborhood spaces encourage walking and bicycling, foster new interpersonal connections, and deepen a sense of community.[17]

In San Francisco, the city has created a new permit that makes greening sidewalks and installing sidewalk gardens much easier and less costly. The time it takes to process the permit as well as the cost of the permit have been significantly reduced compared with earlier sidewalk renewal permits, and the costs goes down with the number of neighbors who together apply for the permit. Small grants have also been provided by the city to support these neighborhood greening projects. And the City of San Francisco's "Pavement to Parks" initiative has fast-tracked the creation of a number of very small (but critical) new spaces, in some cases closing streets. Acknowledging that approximately one-quarter of the land surface in San Francisco is in the form of streets and public rights-of-way, the city created the program to "temporarily reclaim these unused swaths and quickly and inexpensively turn them into new public plazas and parks."[18] There is the possibility that depending on how successful the interventions are, they can become permanent. "Each . . . project is intended to be a public laboratory where the City can work with the community to test the potential of the selected location to be permanently reclaimed as public open space."[19]

New York City's efforts under the leadership of DOT commissioner Janette Sadik-Khan have similarly yielded new urban parks and pedestrian spaces. These include new pedestrian plazas along Broadway, which include new landscaping and seating, and the permanent closure of Times Square to traffic. In announcing the permanent closure, Mayor Bloomberg was bolstered by some striking statistics about reductions in pedestrian and motorist injuries over the eight-month period: Pedestrian injuries in the area fell by 35 percent, and injuries to motorists and passengers fell by 65 percent. A survey of local merchants found that more than two-thirds of the area's retail outfits wanted the project to become permanent.[20]

A number of other places in the city lanes have been closed to car traffic, and new pedestrian spaces and bike lanes have been created in their stead. One new initiative called Summer Streets closes several major thoroughfares in Manhattan, from the Brooklyn Bridge to Central Park, on Sundays in the summer for use by bicyclists and pedestrians. Much of this would not be possible if not for Sadik-Khan designating these changes "pilot projects," which under New York City law means they do not require a vote of approval from the City Council.[21]

Urban agriculture faces a variety of similar regulatory and legal constraints, with poultry and livestock often forbidden under urban zoning regulations. From city to city these restrictions are inconsistent and more a function of historical accident than logic or reasoning. Bees (and beekeeping) are permitted in the city of Toronto, for instance, while chickens are forbidden. Just the reverse is true for New York City.[22] In many cities, efforts are under way to loosen these regulations to make urban agriculture and neighborhood food production easier.

Educating for Urban Biophilia: No Child Left Inside

Educating for urban biophilia must also become a priority. A number of state and local initiatives entitled "Leave No Child Inside" usually involve new funding for a mix of outdoor activities and environmental education.[23] In some states, such as California, proclamations and outdoor bills of rights have been adopted, helping to raise awareness of the child–nature disconnect. Chicago Wilderness, a coalition of more than 240 organizations promoting regional nature conservation, has issued its own Children's Outdoor

Bill of Rights, as part of its own Leave No Child Inside Initiative. This bill of rights holds that "every child should have the opportunity to: discover wilderness . . . camp under the stars . . . follow a trail . . . catch and release fish, frogs and insects . . . climb a tree . . . explore nature in neighborhoods and cities," among other things.[24] The goal of the bill of rights is to "draw attention to the importance of unstructured playtime and other activities and contribute to a culture in which children enjoy and are encouraged to be outside in nature."[25]

Part of the task is to make learning about community and place fun, something that you would want to do and that would compete with the many other life diversions. One especially opportune time to educate citizens about native flora and fauna is when new residents are moving into the neighborhood. They may be especially open to learning about the larger home that they've just joined.

Community maps of various sorts can begin to build a sense of living in a wondrous place by educating citizens about the special and unique nature and ecology nearby. Biophilic community mapping could be done at several scales, such as nature maps at the neighborhood level.[26] The San Francisco organization Nature in the City, a project of the Earth Island Institute, has produced a map of the natural areas and remnant nature in that city that very effectively shows what exists and how to find it. A map could situate the street and neighborhood and even the larger city in its original natural context (where the original creeks and riparian areas were before development and culverts). Also layered onto this map would be the not-so-recent history of a community, including critical information about Native American settlement history. Walking maps that show sites to visit could also help to get citizens to explore their natural community.

An even more strident approach would be to impose some form of (dare I say) mandatory short course about the nature, natural history, and ecology of the community and region. We don't think it unreasonable to require all those wishing to drive an automobile to obtain a license (and to pass a test demonstrating minimum levels of knowledge and competency). Similar testing and licensing is needed to fly an airplane or operate heavy equipment or even to engage in fishing and hunting. One model I had the chance to visit several years ago is the beautiful marine park north of Honolulu, Hawaii, called Hanauma Bay. Before you are permitted to descend onto this pristine beach and coral reef, you are required to watch a nine-minute film about the park, its biodiversity, its fragility, and the standards of care expected of visitors. The film was quite good and effectively conveyed not only helpful information but, more important, a sense of the sacred and unique nature of what was beyond the gate. I don't know if

Figure 5.2 At the natural area of Hanauma Bay, in Honolulu, all visitors must watch a short video about the ecology of the park before they are allowed to enter. Photo credit: Tim Beatley

there is any evidence that this short film has changed the behavior or attitude of visitors, but my hunch is that the mere step of requiring visitors to watch it infuses a heightened reverence about the park they are about to explore.

I'm not sure how we might devise an analogous tool for imparting a similar kind of reverence to new residents of a community or region (would it be a film, as well?), but I think it not an unreasonable request. Could we perhaps institute a requirement for something like a "Caring for Place" certificate that all new homeowners or occupants of apartments might have to obtain—analogous perhaps to a certificate of occupancy—in which a basic understanding of local history, ecology, and sustainable living might be stipulated?

But perhaps the goal should be one of finding ways to nurture deep knowledge about and care for place through everyday life and living. The walk to work, the evening stroll, or the trip to the market or library should ideally reinforce the special qualities of a place, uncovering something at once familiar and comfortable but showing glimpses of the wildness and mystery all around.

There are many things that we do in daily life that are treated as rather unexciting and mundane but could be reconceived as place-strengthening activities. We are told, for instance, to shop for the best value. The ascendance of green values in recent years has questioned these assumptions, suggesting that we as consumers may have ethical and citizenship duties that extend to the realm of shopping—to buy less perhaps, to buy organic foods, to attempt to understand where a product was sourced, and to have at least some degree of sensitivity to its potential environmental impacts. Similar thinking can and should extend to buying on behalf of place and community.

Communities are increasingly finding that programs at coaching residents to live more sustainable lives can be very effective. An organization in my home city of Charlottesville, Virginia, ACCT (Alternatives Community Choices in Transportation), has been running a very successful bike mentoring program that links experienced bicyclists with new or aspiring bicyclists. The one-on-one attention and encouragement (in this case, riding along with the mentee to offer tips and reassurance) helps to get people on bicycles, a biophilic goal. This idea could be extended to community coaches or mentors who facilitate nature walks or nature writing or rock collecting or anything else that involves a new connection with the natural world around us and could benefit from one-on-one teaching.

Overcoming the Cultural and Social Obstacles to Biophilic Cities

Addressing the larger cultural and social obstacles may be significantly harder than addressing regulatory barriers. Even when marvelous green features and resources exist in urban neighborhoods, there is no guarantee that residents—children and adults alike—will actually use them. Limited time, busy schedules, heavily programmed lives, and the growing infringement of technology are some of the obstacles. Some of these might be overcome by the cultivation of "natural social capital," discussed in earlier sections, and the "nudge" and nature coaching ideas. It will likely take a concerted reassessment of priorities and the combined commitment of parents, schools, and employers who understand the ultimate life-enhancing value of time spent outside and in close, daily contact with the natural world.

Richard Louv and others point out that limited time in daily life, especially in the lives of kids, makes connection to nature difficult. Free-ranging kids are not possible in part because their lives are so much more programmed and scheduled than just a generation ago. Louv points to the common practice of homeowners' associations banning the building of tree houses, motivated partly by concerns about legal liability. Perhaps tort reform or further creative efforts at hold-harmless provisions might somewhat reduce the fear of liability. There are, moreover, a variety of green urban and biophilic design elements that are (still) illegal in many cities and states, and efforts should be made to reconsider the virtue of these restrictions. These apply to everything from disconnecting home downspouts to permit rain gardens and on-site stormwater collection, to use of native landscaping. Many traditional zoning codes in cities prohibit biophilic activities such as growing food (in one's yard) and raising chickens, and there is now a movement in many cities to revise these codes to permit such activities (e.g., Milwaukee is currently considering such a green city code). New York City's Green Code Task Force recently released a comprehensive analysis and set of recommendations for code changes in that city, many with implications for biophilic planning and design.[27] Among the suggestions are to remove zoning and regulatory barriers to sustainable technologies like solar energy, require the planting of native plants on city parks and property, prohibit turfgrass in sidewalk planting strips, put into place new requirements for permeable areas in new developments,[28] and create a voluntary program for protecting the city's older trees. As new sensibilities and attitudes and needs about urban nature have emerged, it is time to consider comprehensive rewrites of our urban codes.

Some of the obstacles to wild nature in cities are aesthetic. Native landscaping—in either the public or the private realms—strikes many Americans as unkempt or untidy. While there are maintenance and mowing strategies that can help to counter this (mowing borders to indicate the intentionality of wilder, more natural environments), some green features will simply look out of place or unattractive to Americans raised with turfgrass lawns and hard-surface parking facilities. The recent experience of one southern Californian couple is telling. The couple removed their turfgrass lawn and replaced it with drought-tolerant plants, resulting in a dramatic reduction in water consumption, but instead of praise, they were fined and prosecuted by Orange County officials.[29] Old habits (and visual and aesthetic expectations) die hard, it seems.

There are many larger cultural changes that would be needed to move American cities in the direction of biophilic urbanism. Rethinking the school day to provide greater time for outside play and learning, reducing the extent of the workweek and hours worked, helping to cultivate a walking culture (such as exists in Spain), and reforming work environments so that nature walks and outside respite become standard features of the American workday are all possibilities, but these changes would not be easy or quick to bring about.

Fear is another significant cultural and social factor that significantly impedes our contact with outdoors and nature. Some of this fear—what Richard Louv refers to as the "bogeyman syndrome"—seems driven by concerns by parents about abduction, and as Louv argues, we are doing our children no favors by cocooning them away. Indeed, quite the contrary. And the larger media culture of sensationalist reporting has tended to dramatically overstate these risks of human danger.

On top of this are the fears about nature itself. And again media sensationalism is a part of the problem. A 2009 headline in the Metro section of the *Washington Post* declared "Bats Be Gone!" and was largely a fear-filled piece about the (very small) dangers of rabid bats.[30] There was no mention of their ecological importance and helpful value in controlling insects, or the fascination value of watching and learning about them. And other supposedly responsible media outlets continue to emphasize the danger associated with plants and animals.

The attitudes of wildlife managers and local police officials toward urban wildlife often send a similar message, unfortunately. For example, in Los Angeles, seven coyotes were killed in response to one of them nipping the foot of a sleeping visitor in the city's Griffith Park. It is not clear that the coyotes were an imminent threat to anyone, and in any case killing them (and all of them) was an overreaction. Too often, it seems, rather than enjoying the promise of a potentially exhilarating contact, wildlife and police agencies seek to avoid the potential risk, in knee-jerk fashion. The message sent to the public is (again) unfortunately that such majestic urban residents (the coyote, that is) are a danger, a menace, and should be dealt with accordingly. In the aftermath of the killings it was pointed out that domestic dogs—the dog next door—are a much greater threat to life and safety and account for a much greater number of bites and attacks.[31]

Fear of danger and harm from other humans is, sadly, a more reasonable fear. Personal safety represents a significant and real obstacle to biophilic cities and will require considerable thinking and work to overcome in the future. There is understandable fear, for instance, that leaving windows open to enjoy the evening sounds of summer invites break-ins. Equally true, there are very real dangers to women especially in visiting parks and green areas, disproportionate to the dangers experienced by men. Is it possible to achieve the conditions of a truly biophilic city without tackling the overarching problem of violence against women? Without so doing, the biophilic city becomes a profoundly inequitable city.

There are many steps that could be taken to help create safer parks and natural spaces—remembering Jane Jacobs's famous admonition to create more "eyes on street" would help, and we should employ all the techniques that bring more people to these places. Compactness and density will help generate foot traffic and more eyes. Community policing, further funding of park ranger corps that exist in cities like New York and Los Angeles, and providing many opportunities for group hikes and nature visits would also enhance safety. One interesting effort organized by the city of Anchorage to make it safer to visit its trail system is a program called Trail Watch. Trained volunteers, equipped with cell phones and wearing special armbands, agree to patrol particular trail segments at particular times (devoting at least two hours a week to become a "Trail Ambassador").

New Community Institutions and Capabilities

What new or different institutional and organizational structures are needed in cities to help push a biophilic and green agenda? Cities often have a variety of other organizations and institutions that play (or could play) important roles in growing a more biophilic community. These include botanical gardens, municipal zoos, natural history museums, and conservation groups and consortia.

One interesting question is the extent to which city zoos might help in better promoting these biophilic sensibilities. Traditionally zoos have emphasized exotic animals and biodiversity—imparting more knowledge of distant species than local flora and fauna. There are a few notable exceptions. Local wildlife rehabilitation centers offer some hope for a different, more native approach, as do more locally oriented zoological parks. The Western North Carolina (WNC) Nature Center in Asheville, North Carolina is a positive case in point. Jointly operated by the City of Ashville and Friends of the WNC Nature Center, this facility operates much like a zoo but with exhibits of local fauna. Visitors can howl with coyotes, see precious red wolves that used to roam the region, and see close up many species that might appear at the backdoor, from black bears to raccoons. Ironically, the center was originally the site of a conventional zoo in the Depression era, with elephants and lions and other exotic critters that have little to do with the unique ecology of western North Carolina. The original zoo closed for financial reasons, but the wildlife center that has risen in its place is a different facility entirely, focused essentially on teaching residents about the flora and fauna found not on the African savanna but in and around the woods and open fields and parking lots of Asheville. There is a small

greenhouse structure where visitors can experience local species of butterflies, with bottles of sugar spray to encourage them to land on a hand or an
arm. There are also a number of young adults serving as guides and interns
at this facility, an additional way in which the center educates. Here the center runs the Junior Naturalist Program, where kids twelve to fifteen years
old get to volunteer and be highly engaged in the daily management and
care of the animals. Junior naturalists are expected to give a minimum of
thirty-five hours a week during the summer, so the level of engagement
is considerable and the potential to shape and steer the life course of these
kids is great indeed.[32]

Around the United States there are also new emerging roles for botanical gardens, and some of the larger and more notable ones are rising to
the challenge of educating and engaging residents in understanding urban
nature.

In Richmond, Virginia, the Lewis Ginter Botanical Garden has
taken on the task of growing some of the food its community needs. During the growing season of 2009 it operated, with volunteer help, a kitchen
garden that provided significant amounts of vegetables to the local food
bank, helping to strengthen food security in that region and promote urban
gardening at the same time. By midsummer the garden had already produced more than three thousand pounds of food for the community.

The Cleveland Botanical Garden has been similarly involved in
local food issues, in particular through its Green Corps urban youth program. The garden now operates five "learning farms," in which high school
students (ages fourteen to eighteen) work and earn income from growing food. The gardens range in size from one-quarter acre to three acres.
One of these is located at the Lonnie Burten public housing project, and
this garden alone employs fifteen students. Many of the gardens are funded
and managed cooperatively with other Cleveland organizations (a neighborhood development corporation, commonly). These are leftover lands
in a city that has many vacant sites, as the population of the city has been
in decline. Since 1996, hundreds of students have participated in Green
Corps, many with life-altering effects. As the botanical garden literature
declares, "Green Corps students grow fruits, vegetables and flowers—as well
as job skills, leadership, and a healthier, greener community for themselves
and their neighbors. Ultimately, these young people learn to appreciate the
earth's capacity for abundance and, in the process, begin to realize their own
abundant potential."[33] In addition to working on the farms and learning
about gardening, they receive education in ecology, small business operation, and nutrition and healthy eating. Some of the food is processed, for in-

stance, into Green Corps Salsa (with the distinctive marketing label "Ripe From Downtown").[34]

For fifteen years the Brooklyn Botanic Garden (BBG) has sponsored an innovative "Greenest Block in Brooklyn" contest. An estimated twelve hundred blocks have participated in the contest since it began in 1994, including some half-million residents.[35] The lively competition encourages Brooklynites to "beautify their blocks, build community, and make Brooklyn green."[36] The contest is supported by the BBG's community horticulture program GreenBridge, which among other things offers urban gardening and greening workshops throughout the year and provides free plants, seeds, and compost.

In Philadelphia, the Pennsylvania Horticultural Society (PHS) has played the key role, through its Philadelphia Green program (or "Philly Green"). Founded in 1827, the society now operates a range of urban greening programs including urban tree planting, helping to set up and maintain community gardens and green rooftops, establishing and maintaining new parks in the city, and providing a host of educational programs. The PHS has an impressive sixteen thousand members. In the early 1990s it created a program called Tree Tenders to promote tree planting throughout the city and to teach and train residents how to plant and take care of these trees.[37] The society produces a monthly gardening magazine, *Green Scene*, and organizes a yearly and quite large flower show, the proceeds from which (ticket sales and sponsorships) go to funding the urban greening program.

One of the newest initiatives is an effort to set up model "green neighborhoods" in two parts of the city. Community workshops and meetings have been organized to identify what kinds of greening strategies should be undertaken.[38] Another innovative and unusual effort is its Green City Teachers program, in which Philadelphia area teachers learn how to incorporate greening and horticultural issues into their curriculum and, during summer workshops, receive hands-on training in such things as building a raised-bed school garden. The PHS is a major force in Philadelphia working on behalf of nature and green in the city.

Such nongovernment urban greening and conservation groups can often do things that government agencies or departments find difficult, and in some cases can serve as a check to government actions that work against nature in cities. A case in point is the New York Restoration Project, which actor Bette Midler created in response to plans by then-mayor Rudy Giuliani to sell off many city-owned community gardens.[39] Now a significant force for neighborhood gardening and greening in the city, the organization is, for instance, helping to plant many of the trees under the city's million-tree goal.

The Social Capital of Biophilic Cities

Local conservation and nature groups could play a greater role in educating about and nudging urbanites toward a closer relationship with the nature around them (what I call natural social capital in chapter 1). The Swedish Society for the Conservation of Nature, for instance, has helped to create an innovative program for training and deploying certified nature guides. These guides are put through training about pedagogy and ecology, and those operating in the Stockholm region become certified by the Stock-holm Visitors Board. The funding comes from several sources, including from the local and municipal governments (e.g., Stockholm County) as well as from the Nature Society. The program began with twenty certified na-ture guides in 2004.[40] These guides are now responsible for a series of na-ture visits and walks to important sites in and around the city of Stockholm.

Many national environmental and conservation groups have local or regional affiliates or chapters that often fill many of these same social functions. The Richmond Audubon Society (RAS), for instance, is a local, urban chapter of the National Audubon Society and with some fourteen hundred members is a very active and large group. In any given week there are numerous field trips and site visits and talks, meetings and committee opportunities, chances to volunteer and to be involved in activities such as bird-banding. There is a strong social component to this group, in addition to the educational and advocacy dimensions.[41] Greater emphasis on local or regional chapters (and activities and engagement) is good advice for the mainstream environmental organizations in the country.

The London Wildlife Trust is an important example of a nonprofit organization running biodiversity conservation projects and awareness cam-paigns, coordinating volunteers, bringing nature into the city's schools, and managing a network of fifty-seven nature reserves in that city. And it is an important advocate and voice for nature within and outside the metro area (it is one of forty-seven wildlife trusts around the UK that make up the Royal Society of Wildlife Trusts). The London Wildlife Trust has assumed a special role in encouraging Londoners to rethink and reimagine the nature around them. One current campaign, "Garden for a Living London," en-courages Londoners to commit to taking one of seven steps to naturalize their gardens and greenspaces around their homes. By the trust's estimates there are an incredible 3 million gardens in greater London, comprising some 38,000 hectares of land.[42] And many of the trust's research projects directly engage and involve residents, such as the Stag Beetle project that seeks to make Londoners amateur entomologists by observing and reporting when and where they encounter the beetles, which have been in decline.

The idea of local field studies clubs or natural history clubs is very appealing, and there are some very old examples of this around the country. One of the best examples is the Washington Biologists' Field Club. Formed more than a hundred years ago, this private organization has had a distinguished membership (including, for instance, John Burroughs and Roger Tory Peterson). When the club was founded, its initial members looked for a site that could accommodate their field studies and found Plummers Island, a twelve-acre island in the Potomac River.[43] Only a few miles from the White House, it has been the focus of countless natural studies and research, one of the best-studied parcels of land anywhere. And while the field studies club aims to promote research, it also has a social side, bringing together individuals with a common fascination for nature and encouraging camaraderie and friendship. The spring shad bake and fall oyster roast are important events in the life of the club. The idea of any social group or club focusing its energies and field studies on a specific site over a long time frame is both interesting and admirable.

There are now some newer and more novel nature-oriented clubs, and my view is that the greater the variety, the better. One of my favorites among the more recent social clubs is the Cloud Appreciation Society, based in the UK. The society boasts more than fifteen thousand members, living in some seventy countries, and has an extensive Web site (cloudappreciationsociety.org). They have even produced a manifesto, which among other things admonishes us to "Look up, marvel at the ephemeral beauty, and live life with your head in the clouds!" Although it is a bit whimsical, and at times tongue-in-cheek, there is much merit to the idea of more fully celebrating the beauty and mystery of clouds. The Cloud Appreciation Society recently announced the opening of the world's first "Official Cloudspotting Area"—a beachfront establishment in Lincolnshire, UK, called the Cloud Bar. It boasts a cloud-viewing platform and "cloud menus" to help patrons identify the different types of clouds they see.

I think it is generally true that we don't spend enough time looking up at the sky at nighttime or during the day. Many communities in the United States and around the world have adopted dark-sky lighting standards that mandate new forms of lighting (e.g., full cut-off lights that provide only downward illumination) as a way to reduce light pollution and help to maintain their visual connection to the timeless and wondrous night sky.

Leadership for Biophilic Cities

Imagining cities as profoundly ecological and natural, and working to further strengthen connections of urbanites with nature, also requires leaders—elected officials, community activists, and design professionals, among others—to step forward and to advance and advocate for often bold ideas and ambitious green agendas. Most of the positive stories of emerging biophilic cities told here involve the critical role of one or more committed individuals who have been able to make things happen.

Mayoral leadership, as we have seen, has been essential in a number of larger cities as the green urban agenda is increasingly embraced and understood as a way to enhance quality of life and economic resilience. Mayors in Chicago (Daley), New York (Bloomberg), Los Angeles (Villaraigosa), and San Francisco (Newsom) stand out, but there are many more. In Europe, Mayor Bertrand Delanoë in Paris and former mayor Ken Livingstone in London have done much to enhance outdoor public spaces (e.g., beaches along the Seine in Paris) and to moderate the impact of cars (e.g., congestion pricing and pedestrianizing spaces in London). In Asia, the former mayor of Seoul, South Korea, Lee Myung-bak, is notable for bold urban greening initiatives, and in Latin America, Jaime Lerner (Curitiba, Brazil) and Enrique Peñalosa (Bogotá, Colombia) have played similar roles. Mayors like these can and do make a huge difference.

Some mayors even come to their positions with special knowledge about or concern for urban nature and biodiversity. In 2009, I interviewed the mayor of the northern Australian city of Darwin, Graeme Sawyer. Mayor Sawyer spoke of the pride his constituents have about the nature around them, the green tree frogs and goannas, and came to public service through his volunteer work on amphibians. Sawyer heads the regional chapter of FrogWatch, a national campaign to educate about the importance of frogs and amphibians and the need to control the spread of the nonnative, invasive cane toad. Sawyer's love of nature and biodiversity conservation intersects beautifully with, and has been a pathway toward, public service.

But we have to begin to understand that leadership on green cities can and must happen on many different levels by many different people and that one can assume an important leadership role in ways other than high elected office. Biophilic leaders exist, for instance, at the neighborhood level in the citizen naturalist who organizes a nature walk, the homeowner who replants her yard with native plants and flowers, and the parents who take their kids on weekly hikes and who place importance on teaching their kids to recognize common species of plants and animals in their community.

Teachers can also assume critical leadership roles and often have unusual sway and influence over the children in their charge. Their leadership may take the form of integrating nature into lesson plans, arguing with their superiors for more time outside and the need for outdoor classrooms, or proposing to plant and maintain a raised-bed garden, for instance. And a biophilic city must be a city that invests in training and nurturing and empowering these nonelected leaders in the community.

Important leaders also emerge from the design and planning professions. In San Francisco the personal activism of architect Jane Martin, in creating an entirely new organization PLANT★SF to promote sidewalk gardens and conversion of hardspaces in the city for new nature, is a standout example. The herculean work of Josh David and Robert Hammond to push relentlessly for the creation of the High Line Park in New York City is yet another example. And there are countless other individuals or groups of individuals who have stepped forward at key points to advocate and agitate for an urban greening idea or project. Sometimes they (or their ideas) are met with skepticism ("you want to do what?"), but without their perseverance and drive the work would not have been done. Public officials like my friend and colleague Luis Andrés Orive, in Vitoria-Gasteiz, Spain, were essential in advocating behind the political scenes and working tirelessly on the many details of a greenbelt and world-class nature center for the residents of that city, for instance.

Progress in advancing biophilic cities and in overcoming the obstacles to biophilic urbanism will require many leaders in many places. Such leaders will not only understand the economic and environmental advantages of biophilic cities but will be marked by their infectious curiosity about the nature around them, by their courage in advancing ideas for sharing this curiosity and caring for and repairing the nature around them.

Concluding Thoughts

This chapter argues that movement toward biophilic cities will require, in addition to design or physical intervention, more systemic changes and investments in new local institutions and capacities that will nurture and nudge us toward nature. Single biophilic projects or demonstrations are helpful, but what is needed are new local planning and design codes and incentives that support, encourage, and in some cases mandate biophilic design and planning (e.g., the greenspace factor requirement that some cities, such as Seattle, have already adopted).

There are a host of significant obstacles to biophilic cities, including economic, social, and cultural obstacles, and new institutions and cooperation from existing institutions will be needed to help overcome these. Important biophilic institutions include botanical gardens, natural history museums, and even zoos. Important as well is a robust network of private organizations that help to form the ecological or natural social capital of the city, such as nature clubs, environmental organizations, and municipal programs that combine education about nature and natural history with socializing and friendship building. Leadership on behalf of nature and nature conservation is essential as well but should be viewed more broadly than just leadership by elected officials. Leadership in support of biophilic cities can be expressed by many, from design professionals to neighborhood activists, to individual homeowners who can imagine a greener, more natureful city and see the importance of working toward this goal.

Six

Concluding Thoughts:
Growing the Biophilic City

It is worth repeating a central theme in this book: There is a remarkable amount of nature in and around cities, and in addition to creating more environmentally sustainable urban areas it can and should serve as the foundation for deeper, more meaningful lives—lives lived in closer connection with nature and with each other. It is a different concept of nature from the more Arcadian notions that tend to underpin our national park system, for instance. It is a nature that has been heavily impacted by the human hand yet no less sheltering and restorative of mind and spirit. And increasingly it is a designed nature, as when we seek to include green elements such as green rooftops and vertical gardens.

The extent of the wildness will depend on where in the metropolitan area we are looking, of course: In the very dense core of a large city it will be harder to see it and to nurture it, but easier perhaps on the edge. But cities must increasingly be understood as essential to preserving and restoring nature, for instance, by reducing the size and land area consumed by buildings and hard spaces, and at the same time integrating new nature into those cities (from sidewalk gardens to vertical green walls, to recycling urbanized land into new wildlife habitats) and creating the conditions essential for a biophilic form of living that facilitate and nudge urbanites to live healthier, more physically active outdoor lives. Cities can serve, as my colleague Kristina Hill argues, as "urban arks," places that help to counterbalance the diminished (and diminishing) biodiversity outside of cities.[1]

Partly what is necessary is a significant popular shift in the way we view cities. On the shallowest level we still see cities and urban environments as devoid of nature, places we need to quickly escape if we don't want to live our lives in a world of concrete and asphalt. There are too many urban environments that are indeed seemingly quite bleak and need profound retooling. But as the stories and initiatives described in this book show, there is much nature already here, in the midst of dense urban buildings and environments. In fact, it is everywhere around us, if we look: above, below, in, and around the buildings and neighborhoods where we live. In some cases, it is leftover nature, such as in San Diego's canyons; in others, it is designed nature, such as a rooftop garden or bioswale. In still other cases, it is the indomitable nature and natural forces that follow us wherever we live, even in cities: the breezes and climate and weather, the migratory birds, the diversity of all the microwilderness that exists around us. We must begin to move into a deeper, more profound understanding of cities as nature, as wondrous and significant and valuable as those in the most pristine national parks. As our planet continues its march to cities, this will be an increasingly important challenge for us to tackle.

Most of us in urban planning argue for the essentiality of cities. The way we design and live in cities is critical to our response to climate change and our future global sustainability. Cities are not just an unstoppable force but a positive trend, one that portends a more sustainable set of future conditions.

Dense cities offer our best hope for living low-carbon lives but also can be designed and managed in ways that make them resilient to changes in climate—the many steps outlined here for moving cities toward greater biophilia will also help to make cities more resilient. Strategies for urban greening and for enhancing urban ecology, whether through a green roof-top or a sidewalk garden, will also serve to reduce urban heat, better conserve water, and manage stormwater runoff and flooding, among other impacts. Many of the urban and neighborhood greening strategies and projects profiled here also help to promote social contact, to build a sense of community, and to nurture friendships, and these forms of social capital will do much in turn to build social resilience. Protecting and restoring larger elements of urban green infrastructure, say, coastal wetlands, will help in adaptation to severe weather events and sea level rise.

Urban populations represent a tremendous potential force in the conservation of nature, urban and otherwise, and an immense pool of labor and volunteerism that might be harnessed on behalf of nature, and we should always remember this. The call for biophilic cities and biophilic urban neighborhoods is not a theoretical notion but a practical reality in many places. And as these many city and neighborhood examples demonstrate, it is indeed possible to combine urban living and life close to nature. Cities already harbor much more nature than we commonly acknowledge, and there are now a host of creative planning and design tools, techniques, and concepts that can be applied to make urban neighborhoods greener and more biophilic. A sustainable future will by necessity require an urban future, I believe, but this does not (indeed, cannot) mean that this future is one that is disconnected and detached from nature and natural systems. The choice, as that *Washington Post* real estate advertisement depicts, between

Figure 6.1 An eastern gray tree frog, held by the author. Photo credit: Tim Beatley

city and nature is a false choice and an unnecessary and outdated dichotomy. Biophilic cities and biophilic urbanism transcend this dichotomy and present a compelling new vision for a rapidly urbanizing world.

I have advocated a comprehensive and holistic notion for advancing and promoting biophilia. It extends, and has to extend, beyond the building or residence. Biophilic urbanism and design must occur at all scales, from room or rooftop to region. And it is multilayered, with biophilic features at different scales reinforcing our biophilic sensibilities.

Curiosity is an essential virtue that needs valuing and cultivating in cities. It is intrinsic to human beings and human spirit, but like other muscles requires vigorous use and exercise. Many of the programs and organizations profiled here aim, in one way or another, to nudge and grow that culture of curiosity, of mindfulness and caring about the life and nature around us. Cities must be designed to provide ready outlets and rewards for even greener. Urban neighborhoods can encourage and facilitate curiosity by designing spaces that allow exploration, elicit questions and probing, or provide us with the means to deepen this curiosity (whether a portable microscope or a pack of garden seeds)..

Perhaps we should also emphasize the public health dimensions of biophilic cities more than we currently do. In this regard, my UVA colleague Tanya Denckla Cobb has had a brilliant idea of extending the nutritional perspective of the food pyramid—for decades a tool for understanding what kinds of food children and adults should be eating and in what basic proportions—to include the idea of nature and contact with nature. She has called it the "nature pyramid," suggesting that there are many

forms of daily nature needed in a city. The lower levels of the pyramid are
the equivalent of the daily vegetables and fruits we need to be healthy. At
the top of the nature pyramid are the more infrequently visited places of
nature—Yosemite, perhaps, or other national parks—certainly important for
deeper, more intense nature experiences, but which (like meat and sweets)
shouldn't and can't make up the bulk of one's diet. The nature pyramid is
not a perfect tool for thinking about nature, but it does suggest that there
might be something equivalent to nutrition—perhaps we should begin to
speak in terms of what the minimum daily requirements for nature are.

Just as we are fully appreciating how essential contact with nature
is in our lives, much of it is under assault. The discouraging news is that
nature is in decline almost everywhere in the world, the results of the pervasive impacts of climate change, population growth, resource extraction,
development, and various other human impacts. This actually increases the
importance of cities as biological reservoirs and venues for ecological restoration and repair. And a fully engaged biophilic populace represents a potential
army of individuals and groups who can work toward these ends, as well as
help to get a better handle on the extent and nature of the impacts on and
changes experienced by natural systems locally and around the world. Cities
represent large potential pools of citizen scientists who could help in many
ways to track and monitor changes. The significant shifting of North American bird populations (it is estimated that some 60% have shifted their ranges
northward[2]) was detected and demonstrated through citizen-collected bird
observations, for instance, so such citizen scientists can make a real difference.
And we must not be complacent in celebrating the small victories in cities
without also working hard (politically and scientifically) to understand and
address the very severe threats facing urban and nonurban nature alike.
Viewing and enjoying and celebrating Mexican free-tailed bats, as in Austin,
Texas, must also be connected with solving the mysteries of the deadly
white-nose syndrome that is wreaking havoc, especially on eastern bat species.

While most of the focus of this book has been on strategies for
integrating nature at home (in our home cities, that is), it is important to
understand that a biophilic city and its inhabitants ought also to be very
engaged and interested in the larger world. Cities, as political and social en -
tities, must become a larger force in the world in support for biodiversity
conservation by actively restoring and shepherding over both the nature
within their borders and the larger global and planetary nature that urbanites affect through consumption patterns and lifestyle decisions and sometimes municipal policy.

Municipal leaders can do much—from forging their own city-
to-city agreements and treaties to conserve and protect about biodiversity,
to adopting stricter procurement policies that reduce impacts on ecosystems

and species in other parts of the world, to instituting policies and projects that reduce greenhouse gas emissions and thus some of the most serious long-term impacts imposed on our planetary home.

There are a variety of important research questions about designing and planning biophilic cities that can and should be pursued. We still have, for instance, relatively little knowledge of the cumulative recuperative and healing powers of urban nature. How do the many smaller green features in a city or urban neighborhood contribute to our closeness with nature, and what are the interactive effects? Is access to a large forest more effective than having a neighborhood full of smaller green features, such as street trees and green rooftops? There are a host of research questions that relate to how effective our biophilic strategies in fact are—what are the most effective planning and policy means for getting people outside? What will it take to nudge urban populations to adopt a more outdoor, nature-oriented lifestyle? Our very understanding of the science and ecology of cities remains quite limited, so there is much work to be done here as well. New research is needed to better understand the biology and lifecycles of urban fauna, and how they change or are modified by urban settings (e.g., think of coyotes), as well as the management implications therein. There are many, almost countless research questions and opportunities that arise from the agenda of biophilic cities.

How do we know when we've been successful at achieving or advancing the biophilic city? How we know when we have succeeded in growing a sense of curiosity in a city or larger society remains a question and a part of the larger endeavor of measuring and taking stock of the extent to which a city and its residents can be said to be biophilic. I've offered some possible indicators and proxies in earlier chapters, but it remains a methodological challenge. How do we know if residents of a city are truly curious, and how do we know how curious they are about the natural world (or other things) compared with residents of other cities? Could we even ignite a friendly competition (in the vein of place-rated studies) between cities to see which can be or become the most curious? Assessing the curiosity of residents of a city is an interesting challenge. Attitudinal surveys would be one standard approach, but perhaps we need to be cleverer about this: setting up a field experiment to see how often passersby stop to watch a hawk or peregrine falcon or the extent to which passersby are interested in learning about an impromptu display of urban wildlife or native plants (e.g., what percentage stop and ask questions?).[3] Some individuals are naturally more curious than others, but we can be encouraged and supported to be more or less curious, and a biophilic city is one in which such questions are asked.

There are many tensions and conflicts in the biophilic cities agenda that need to be addressed. What, for instance, is the attitude toward nonnative and invasive species in biophilic cities? Are there sometimes conflicts between different biophilic design strategies, and if so, how and in what ways are they resolved? When does biophilic urban design become a form of greenwashing—for example, the installation of a green wall argued for as a compensatory measure for the loss of larger nature elements or greenspace in the city because of new construction? The development of green building and landscape certification systems (notably LEED [Leadership in Energy and Environmental Design] and, most recently, the Sustainable Sites Initiative) offers some hope that we might be able to judge more systematically how biophilic a structure or site is and to distinguish between hype and reality. This is a positive step and has undoubtedly encouraged incorporation of biophilic features. But there are many sustainable or green buildings that are quite biologically or biophilically sterile and uninspiring, and we could do a better job in strengthening the presence of active nature. And until recently there have been few measures that help us think about and assess biophilia at the broader city and regional levels. This is changing. One interesting effort, Local Action for Biodiversity (LAB), jointly run by ICLEI–Local Governments for Sustainability and the World Conservation Union, is working to develop a rating system for judging a city's commitment to biodiversity, and it includes some of the measures I have described in chapter 3 in characterizing what a biophilic city is (e.g., amounts of greenspace and nature in the city, governance structure, budget). While still in a pilot stage (twenty cities are participating initially) and not fully capturing all of the ways in which cities can be biophilic, it is nonetheless promising as a way for cities to see where they stand, how they stack up to other cities, and what is possible in other places. It should also assist city officials in seeing the whole—understanding all the different factors that help shape biophilic places and the different commitments necessary, from budgetary and educational to spatial planning, and how they might fit together.[4] But there is still much work that will need doing, much additional writing, thinking, and research, and it is my hope that biophilic cities will gel and come together as a legitimate and important subject for the future work of planners and design scholars.

What nature means, or could mean, in highly urbanized settings remains to be more fully explored and debated. Eric Sanderson, author of *Mannahatta*, argues that cities, certainly cities like New York, can never be expected to harbor populations of large mammals, as they once did.[5] Yet nature and wildness are to be seen in more than the obvious large species of animals. Urban nature includes the small and even microscopic, from lichen and ants to the larger realms of weather and even the night sky, much more, and much more interesting, than the usual understandings of nature.

Who is primarily responsible for advancing or advocating or working on behalf of biophilic urbanism remains a question. The simple answer is that many different people and organizations can make a difference. As the stories contained in this book (and the film *The Nature of Cities*) demonstrate, this is an area where much can productively happen through direct personal and neighborhood intervention. Sidewalks can partially make way for gardens and native plants, new parks can be created from parking and roadway spaces in cities, and forgotten canyons and other forgotten islands of urban nature can be captured and stewarded over by neighborhood groups and Friends organizations. The design and planning professions can also help in important ways, as the role of pro bono design work in cities like San Francisco have shown. Creating more biophilic cities will also require political leadership, of course, and there are now strong indications that politicians are able to reap political benefits from support for green projects.

There are many obstacles to achieving biophilic cities and neighborhoods, and many distractions in modern life steer us far afield from nature. Such technological distractions as television, computers, and iPhones are often seen as significant continuing factors in our growing disconnection with the natural world. But might this technology also help to reconnect us? Online bird, plant, and fungi guidebooks are increasingly common today, and a Vermont company recently announced availability of a new iPhone application that will deliver thousands of bird and plant images to users, including more than two thousand bird calls.[6] That should help make it easier and perhaps more fun to be on the lookout for and identify the life around us in cities.

And more technology is on the way. Perhaps we can imagine a time when the smart phone can be waved across that tree or forest or natural features, perhaps even focused on the bird flying by, and immediately displaying the species name and other information about it. This is an example of what is now referred to as "augmented reality," forms of technology that involve the "layering of virtual imagery and information over a real-world environment."[7] As futurist Paul Saffo notes, "We're going to have lots of augmented reality in the future. . . . Everything you carry will have much more awareness about where it is and what's around it, whether you are interested or not."[8] But perhaps it's the real nature, the real reality that needs emphasizing, no "augmentation" required. Whether we like it or not, I suspect this is the new world, and developing applications that connect and teach us about the natural world around us may be essential, if only to prevent our kids and culture from becoming even more detached.

Perhaps office workers (or residents of a neighborhood) could be directed to the nearest park or trail or natural area, locating nearby nature that might otherwise be hidden from view or a few minutes' walk away. One could imagine an electronic device that might be set to a kind of iPod shuffle, offering a new walking route to try each day at lunch or on the way home from one's bus stop. Google Maps and seemingly ubiquitous GPS units are now commonly used to find directions and plan travel routes, and they could be more cleverly used to guide us to the nature nearby. Walk Scores have now been calculated for much of the United States and are commonly used by real estate agents in showing and selling property, and increasingly by new residents to identify attractive neighborhoods in which to live. The Walk Score includes distance to parks, but perhaps a more focused greenness or neighborhood nature score ought to also be delivered as an important complementary measure of the desirable qualities of an urban neighborhood (only one biophilic amenity, parks, is included in its algorithm; no other green elements are taken into account). The technology that helps us find our way in cars, then, or helps us locate a restaurant in which to have dinner, might also help us to find and more fully appreciate the nature around us. But of course it is a double-edged sword, and it is not clear that mediation by any form of electronic device will instill a deep affection for and concern about nature.

There are many ways in which modern technology could be helpful, from easily updated, Web-based field guides to the use of sound equipment to bring outdoor sounds indoors. Even such devices as portable digital microscopes or new-generation camera traps can be used in promising ways. Many of these possibilities could be quite creative and could dovetail with other sustainability ideas and products. For instance, perhaps new smart energy meters being sold and installed in many homes (with Prius-like displays that can even visually indicate energy consumption in terms of dollars expended) could also be used to convey biophilic information, for instance, alerting the family to the height of raptor migration in the area or advising the family about an unusually promising night sky or skygazing opportunity.

Much of the task in the future, certainly for those in city planning and urban design, will be in offering an alternative vision of cities and urban neighborhoods. As Stephen Kellert of Yale University has said, "We need to do more than just avoid all the bad things that we have done in terms of our adverse effects on natural systems. We also have to create the context for thriving, for development, for meaningful exchange with the world around us, and the people around us. And for that we need to restore that sense of relationship with the natural world which has always been the cradle of our creativity."[9] That vision will be of dense, sustainable, walkable cities and places that are also full of nature and are profoundly restorative, magical, and wondrous.

Endnotes

Preface

1. Stephen Kellert, Judith Heerwagen, and Marty Mador, eds., *Biophilic Design: The Theory, Science and Practice of Bringing Buildings to Life*, Hoboken, NJ: John Wiley, 2008.

2. E. O. Wilson, *The Creation: An Appeal to Save Life on Earth*, New York: Norton, 2006.

Chapter 1

1. E. O. Wilson, "Biophilia and the Conservation Ethic," in Stephen Kellert and E. O. Wilson, *The Biophilia Hypothesis,* Washington, DC: Island Press, 1993, pp. 31–41.

2. Richard Louv, *Last Child in the Woods: Saving Our Children from Nature Deficit Disorder*, Chapel Hill, NC: Algonquin Press, 2005.

3. Paul Gruchow, *Grass Roots: The Universe of Home (The World as Home)*, Minneapolis: Milkweed Editions, 1995.

4. E. O. Wilson, in Kellert and Wilson, *The Biophilia Hypothesis*, 1993, p. 32.

5. Stephen Kellert, *Building for Life: Designing and Understanding the Human–Nature Connection,* Washington, DC: Island Press, 2006, p. 4.

6. Roger Ulrich, "View through a Window May Influence Recovery from Surgery, *Science* 224 (April 27, 1984):421.

7. MIND, "Ecotherapy: The Green Agenda for Mental Health," MIND weekly report, May 2007. The study concludes the following: "The new research . . . shows green exercise has particular benefits for people experiencing mental distress. It directly benefits mental health (lowering stress and boosting self-esteem), improves physical health (lowering blood pressure and helping to tackle obesity), provides a source of meaning and purpose, helps to develop skills and form social connections" (p. 28).

8. See T. Hartig, M. Mang, and G. W. Evans, "Restorative Effects of Natural Environmental Experience," *Environment and Behavior* 33 (1991):3–26; T. Hartig and H. Staats, "The Need for Psychological Restoration as a Determinant of Environmental Preferences," *Journal of Environmental Psychology* 26 (2006):215–226.

9. Agnes E. Van den Berg, Terry Hartig, and Henk Staats, "Preference for Nature in Urbanized Societies: Stress, Restoration, and the Pursuit of Sustainability," *Journal of Social Issues* 63 (no.1, 2007):88–89.

10. Sjerp DeVries, Robert A. Verheij, Peter P. Groenewegen, and Peter Spreeu-wenberg, "Natural Environments—Healthy Environments? An Exploratory Analy-sis of the Relationship between Greenspace and Health," *Environment and Planning A* 35 (2003):1726.

11. Ibid.

12. Thomas Sick Nielsen and Karsten Bruun Hansen, "Do Green Areas Affect Health? Results from a Danish Survey on the Use of Green Areas and Health Indi-cators," *Health and Place* 13 (2007):839–850.

13. Peter Schantz and Erik Stigell, "Are Green Elements Principal Pull Factors for Physical Activity?" The Research Unit for Movement, Health and Environ-ment, The Swedish School for Sport and Health Sciences, Stockholm, summary of a presentation, supplied by the author.

14. Ben Fried, "New Yorkers Reap Health Benefits from Walking," found at www.streetblog.org, December 3, 2009.

15. For a good discussion see, for example, Kristin L. Getter and D. Bradley Rowe, "The Role of Extensive Green Roofs in Sustainable Development," *HortScience* 41 (no. 5, 2006):1276–1286.

16. The Trust for Public Land, "Parks and Playground Use Up in Down Economy," found at www.tpl.org, August 2009.

17. David Futrelle, "Putting a Price on Walkability," *CNN Money*, August 22, 2009. See also Carol Coletta, "Walking the Walk," found at www.ceosforcities.org/work/walkingthewalk, accessed May 27, 2010.

18. Andrew Revkin, "Peeling Back Pavement to Expose Watery Havens," *New York Times*, July 16, 2009, found at www.nytimes.com/2009/07/17/world/asia/17daylight.html?_r=2&pagewanted=1&ref=science, accessed May 27, 2010.

19. Anne Schwartz, "Good Parks Are Good for the Economy," *Gotham Ga-zette*, June 24, 2009.

20. Robert Costanza, Octavio Pérez-Maqueo, M. Luisa Martinez, Paul Sut-ton, Sharolyn J. Anderson, and Kenneth Mulder, "The Value of Coastal Wetlands for Hurricane Protection," *AMBIO: A Journal of the Human Environment* 37 (no. 4, 2008):241–248.

21. Anne Schwartz, "Good Parks Are Good for the Economy," *Gotham Ga-zette,* June, 2009.

22. Ryerson University, *Report on the Environmental Benefits and Costs of Green Roof Technology for the City of Toronto*, prepared for the City of Toronto, Department of Architecture, Ryerson University, Toronto, October 31, 2005.

23. See The Greening of Detroit, at www.greeningogdetroit.com/9_0_about_us.php, accessed December 21, 2009.

24. USC Center for Sustainable Cities, *Green Visions Plan*, August 2008, found at www.greenvisionsplan.net.

25. See Elisabeth Kals, Daniel Shumacher, and Leo Montada, "Emotional Af-finity toward Nature as a Motivational Basis to Protect Nature," *Environment and Behavior* 31 (no. 2, March 1999):178–202.

26. See discussion of this in Timothy Beatley, *Planning for Coastal Resilience,* Washington, DC: Island Press, 2009, chapter 2.

27. Specifically, participants were asked to participate in a decision task called a "funds distribution" task; see p. 1322 for a full explanation.

28. Netta Weinstein, Andrew K. Przybylski, and Richard M. Ryan, "Can Nature Make Us More Caring? Effects of Immersion in Nature on Intrinsic Aspirations and Generosity," *Personality and Social Psychology Bulletin* 35 (no. 10, October 2009):1315–1329.

29. Ibid., p. 1316.

30. For a good review of this issue and current research, see Kenneth R. Ginsberg, "The Importance of Play in Promoting Healthy Child Development and Maintaining Strong Parent–Child Bonds," *American Academy of Pediatrics* 119 (no. 1, January 2007):82–191.

31. Victoria Rideout, Ulla G. Foehr, and Donald F. Roberts, *Generation M2: Media in the Lives of 8- to 18-Year-Olds,* a Kaiser Family Foundation Study, January 2010, p. 2.

32. Robert Pyle, *The Thunder Tree: Lessons from an Urban Wildland,* Boston: Houghton-Mifflin, 1993, p. 146.

33. Ibid.

34. Lauran Neergaard, "Obesity Rates Rising, Mississippi's Still Fattest," *Washington Post,* July 1, 2009.

35. Live Science, "Lack of Vitamin D in Children 'Shocking,'" found at www .livescience.com/health/090803-vitamin-d-children.html, accessed December 10, 2009.

36. Rachel Carson, "Help Your Child to Wonder," *Woman's Home Companion,* July 1956, p. 46.

37. Ibid., p. 48.

38. Ibid.

39. See Elisabeth Kals, Daniel Shumacher, and Leo Montada, "Emotional Affinity toward Nature as a Motivational Basis to Protect Nature," *Environment and Behavior* 31 (no. 2, March 1999):178–202.

40. Personal communication, University of Adelaide.

41. See Jennifer Wolch, "Zoöpolis," *Capitalism Nature Socialism* 7 (no. 2, June 1996):21–47; Mona Seymour and Jennifer Wolch, "Toward Zoöpolis? Innovation and Contradiction in a Conservation Community," *Journal of Urbanism* 2 (no. 3, November 2009):215–236.

42. Jennifer Wolch, 1996, p. 29.

Chapter 2

1. The next two paragraphs draw heavily from Beatley, "Towards Biophilic Cities," in Kellert, Heerwegen and Mador, eds., *Biophilic Design,* Hoboken, NJ: John Wiley and Sons, 2008.

2. Eric Chivian and Aaron Bernstein, eds., *Sustaining Life: How Human Health Depends on Biodiversity,* Oxford: Oxford University Press, 2008.

3. "Dimming Lights Saves Birds, Study Says," *Chicago Tribune,* May 9, 2002, section 1: "Field Museum scientists collected birds killed after striking the windows

and found that turning off the interior lights or pulling drapes reduced deaths by 83 percent."

4. City of Toronto, *Bird-Friendly Development Guidelines,* March 2007.

5. City of Toronto, "Bird-Friendly Development Rating System and Acknowledgement Program," found at www.toronto.ca/lightsout/guidelines.htm, accessed May 27, 2010.

6. Theresa Boyle, "These Buildings Are for the Birds," *Toronto Star,* May 4, 2007; for more about birds in that city, see Gerald McKeating, *Birds of Toronto,* Edmonton, Alberta, Canada: Lone Pine Publishing, 1990.

7. New York City Department of Environmental Protection, "Peregrine Falcons in New York City," found at nyc.gov/html/dep/html/news/falcon.shtml, accessed October 16, 2009.

8. "Peregrine Falcons Nesting in Richmond," in *Local Bird News,* Richmond Audubon Society, found at www.richmondaudubon.org/NewsPeregrine.html, accessed December 10, 2009.

9. Jane McKay, "San Francisco Is a Bird Watcher's Paradise," *San Francisco Chronicle,* February 23, 2009.

10. New Housing, New York Legacy Project, "Phipps-Rose-Dattner-Grimshaw Selected to Develop City-Owned Site in South Bronx," press release, January 17, 2007.

11. Richard Preston, *The Wild Trees: A Story of Passion and Daring,* New York: Random House, 2007.

12. Irwin M. Brodo, Sylvia Duran Sharnoff, and Stephen Sharnoff, *Lichens of North America,* New Haven, CT: Yale University Press, 2001.

13. Jennifer Amie, "Surprising Symbionts: The Unusual Biology of Lichens," *University of Minnesota News,* November 27, 2007.

14. H. J. M. Sipman puts the numbers at 290 and 308, respectively. See Sipman, "Tropical Urban Lichens: Observations from Singapore," *Blumea—Biodiversity, Evolution and Biogeography of Plants* 54 (nos. 1–3, October 2009):297–299.

15. For example, Dobson, *Guide to Urban Lichens,* Field Studies Centre, UK, 2006.

16. For more on the biology of tardigrades, see Ian M. Kinchin, *The Biology of Tardigrades,* Surrey, UK: Ashgate Publishers, 1994. There have been relatively few studies of tardigrades in cities; see the following: Peluffa, Rocha, and Peluffa, "Species Diversity and Morphometrics of Tardigrades in a Medium-Sized City in the Neotropical Region: Santa Ross," *Animal Biodiversity and Conservation* 30 (2007): 43–51; Peluffo, Peluffo, and Rocha, "Tradigrade Distribution in a Medium-Sized City of Central Argentina," *Hydrobiologia* 558 (2006):141–150.

17. Species Distribution Project, Tardigrade Facts, Illinois Wesleyan University, found at www.iwu.edu/~tardisp/tardigrade_facts.html, accessed November 21, 2009.

18. John H. Crowe, Folkert A. Hoekstra, and Lois M. Crowe, "Anhydrobiosis," *Annual Review of Physiology* 54 (1992):579–599.

19. See, for instance, Reinhardt M. Kristensen, Łukasz Michalczyk, and Łukasz Kaczmarek, "The First Record of the Genus *Bryodelphax* (Tardigrada: Hetero-

tardigrada: Echiniscidae) from Easter Island, Rapa Nui (Pacific Ocean, Chile) with the Description of a New Species, *Bryodelphax aaseae*," *Zootaxa* 2343:45–56 (2010); Łukasz Kaczmarek and Łukasz Michalczyk, "Two New Species of Macrobiotidae, *Macrobiotus szeptyckii (harmsworthi* Group) and *Macrobiotus kazmierskii (hufelandi* Group) from Argentina," *Acta Zoologica Cracoviensia* 52B(1–2):87–99, Kraków, June 30, 2009; Łukasz Kaczmarek, and Łukasz Michalczyk, "New Records of Water Bears (*Tardiigrada, Eutardiigrada*) from Romania" *Studia Universitatis* 18 (suppl., 2008); Peter Degma, Łukasz Michalczyk, and Łukasz Kaczmarek, "*Macrobiotus derkai,* a New Species of Tardigrada (Eutardigrada, Macrobiotidae, *huziori* Group) from the Colombian Andes (South America)," *Zootaxa* 1731 (2008):1–23; Cheon Young Chang, Łukasz Kaczmarek, Ji Min Lee, and Łukasz Michalczyk, "*Pseudobiotus spinifer,* a New Tardigrade Species (Eutardigrada: Hypsibiidae) from Nakdong River, South Korea, with a Redescription of *P. vladimiri* Biserov, Dudichev & Biserova," *Zoological Science* 24 (2007): 623–629.

20. For example, see Q. Schiermeier, "'Rain-Making' Bacteria Found around the World," *Nature News*, February 28, 2008; K. A. Pratt et al., "Detection of Biological Particles in Cloud Ice Crystals," *Nature Geoscience*, May 17, 2009.

21. See www.darksky.org.

22. For a discussion of some of the threats to the survival of this tree, see Corey Kilgannon, "In Obscurity, The Tallest and Oldest New Yorker," *New York Times*, March 27, 2004.

23. Stockholm County, "Outings Guide to 33 Protected Natural Areas in Stockholm County," undated, Stockholm, Sweden.

24. Ibid., p. 39.

25. New York City Department of Parks and Recreation, "Alley Pond Park," found at www.nycgovparks.org/parks/alleypondpark, accessed September 10, 2009.

26. See Leslie Day, *Field Guide to the Natural World of New York City,* Johns Hopkins Press, Baltimore, Maryland, 2007. See also www.nycgovparks.org/sub_about/parks_divisions/nrg/forever_wild/foreverwild_home.html.

27. See Gateway National Recreational Area, www.nps.gov/gate/naturescience/animals.htm, accessed May 27, 2010. For a review of climate change impacts on and implications for Jamaica Bay, see Columbia University, *Long-Term Resource Management under a Changing Climate,* 2009, found at www.nps.gov/gate/parknews/long-term-resource-management-under-a-changing-climate.htm, accessed May 27, 2010.

28. At the very end of the Canyonlands white paper, it identifies "next steps," for the most part very sensible and perhaps obvious things that need to happen to elevate the visibility of the solid advice of "broadening the constituency" in support of canyons and canyon preservation. This seems an essential step. More specifically, the report says, "Broaden the constituency for canyon preservation by raising awareness regarding the essential quality of life benefits derived from canyons. A good starting point is to organize speaking tours with residents and community planning groups throughout San Diego. With respect to groups representing different priorities, it is necessary to identify common ground and interests in order to build broad coalitions. This will involve articulating and quantifying relationships

between the economy, quality of life, and the canyons." San Diego Civic Solutions, 2006, p. 20.

29. "Nature in the City: A Guide to San Francisco's Natural Heritage," July 2007, Nature in the City, a project of Earth Island Institute, San Francisco.

30. Peter Brastow, Nature in the City, "Journal," Earth Island Institute, undated.

31. Lucy Hutcherson, "Chicago Wilderness: A Collaborative Model for Urban Conservation," in Ted Trzyna, ed., *The Urban Imperative: Urban Outreach Strategies for Protected Area Agencies*, Sacramento: InterEnvironment, California Institute of Public Affairs, 2003, p. 138.

32. Chicago Wilderness Consortium, *Atlas of Biodiversity*, Chicago: Chicago Region Biodiversity Council, 2001.

33. Chicago Wilderness Consortium, *Biodiversity Recovery Plan*, Chicago: Chicago Wilderness Consortium, 1999.

34. Larry Rizzo, *Kansas City Wildlands*, Jefferson City, Missouri Department of Conservation, 2001.

35. Ibid., p. 49.

36. Erik Gleibermann, "Grab a Latte and Bike but Watch Out for Bears," *Boston Globe*, February 15, 2009, p. M3 travel; Yereth Rosen, "The Moose Babysitter," *Christian Science Monitor*, July 19, 2007, p. 20 features, currents.

37. See "Anchorage Trails System Adds to Quality of Life," at www.americantrails.org.

38. Alaska Division of Wildlife Conservation, "Living with Wildlife in Anchorage," Anchorage, Alaska, 2000, p. 39.

39. A study of 500 coyote scat samples in Calgary, Canada found that only about 1 percent had the remains of domestic animals. Nick Lewis, "Research Defends City's Wiley Coyotes," *Calgary Herald*, June 26, 2009.

40. "Coyotes within City Limits," a segment of the radio show *Which Way LA*, KCRW, November 2009.

41. King County, Washington, *King County Biodiversity Report*, 2008, p. 57.

42. Peter Brastow, "Urban Nature and Franciscan Natural Resources Facts and FAQs," Nature in the City, found at www.natureinthecity.org/sf%20nature%20factsandfaq.pdf, accessed May 27, 2010.

43. Walter R. Schinkel, "The Nest Architecture of the Florida Harvester Ant, Pogonomyrmes," *Journal of Insect Science* 4 (2004):21.

44. Max Planck Institute, "Hairy Feet Stick Better to Wet Ceilings," press release, November 9, 2005, found at www.mpg.de/english/illustrations Documentation/documentation/pressReleases/2005/pressRelease20051109/, accessed February 26, 2010.

45. E. O. Wilson, *The Creation: An Appeal to Save Life on Earth*, New York: Norton, 2006, p. 18.

46. Ibid., p. 32.

47. Morgan E. Helm, "Denver's Street Smart Prairie Dogs," October 2, 2009, found at www.smithsonianmag.com/science-nature/Denvers-Street-Smart-Prairie-Dogs.html.

48. Jill Bolte Taylor, *My Stroke of Insight: A Brain Scientist's Personal Journey*, New York: Plume, 2009, p. 20.

49. For more about spring peepers, see www.dnr.state.md.us/features/spring _peepers.asp.

50. I first learned of this observation and of the Kroodsma book from an excellent column by Margaret Wooster, "Winter Solstice Is the First Day of Spring," in *River Currents*, December 2009, an e-newsletter of the Buffalo Niagara Riverkeepers.

51. Peter R. Marler and Hans Slabbekoorn, *Nature's Music: The Science of Birdsong*, San Diego: Elsevier Academic Press, 2004.

52. U.S. Army Corps of Engineers, "Welcome to Devonian Fossil Gorge," found at www.mvr.usace.army.mil/coralville/default.htm, accessed May 27, 2010.

53. Tom Dean, "Finding Devonian," in *Living with Topsoil: Tending Spirits, Cherishing Land*, North Liberty, IA: Ice Cube Press, 2004.

54. Leslie Day, *Field Guide to the Natural World of New York City*, Baltimore: Johns Hopkins University Press, 2001.

55. Ibid., p. 22.

56. Eric Sanderson, *Mannahatta: A Natural History of New York City*, New York: Abrams, 2009.

57. Ibid., p. 138.

58. Ibid., p. 204.

59. Ibid., p. 242. By 2409, Sanderson speculates, people will live "in a necklace of unique and extraordinary cities on only 36 percent of the land (assuming the same density as modern Manhattan), surrounded by farms, wildlands, and a restored and thriving estuary, with boundaries redrawn by climate change."

Chapter 3

1. Peter Schantz and Erik Stigell, "Are Green Elements Principal Pull Factors for Physical Activity?" The Research Unit for Movement, Health and Environment, The Swedish School for Sport and Health Sciences, Stockholm, summary of a presentation, supplied by the author.

2. Stephen Kellert interview, *The Nature of Cities* film, 2009.

3. Janine M. Benyus, *Biomimicry: Innovation Inspired by Nature*, New York: Harper Perennial, 1997.

4. William McDonough and Michael Braungart, *Cradle to Cradle: Remaking the Way We Make Things*, New York: North Point Press, 2002.

5. Janine Benyus, "A Good Place to Settle: Biomimicry, Biophilia, and the Return of Nature's Inspiration to Architecture," in Stephen Kellert, Judith Herrwegen, and Marty Mador, eds., *Biophilic Design*, Hoboken, NJ: John Wiley and Sons, 2008, pp. 27–42.

6. Winifred Bird, "Natural by Design," *Japan Times*, August 24, 2008.

7. See C. Majidi et al., "High Friction from a Stiff Polymer Using Micro-Fiber Arrays," *Physical Review Letters* 97 (no. 076103, August 18, 2006).

8. Quoted in "Michigan State Collaboration Spawns Robotic Fish to Monitor Water Quality," *MSU News*, November 2, 2009, found at news.msu.edu/story/7057/, accessed March 3, 2010.

9. Ecopurer, "Reduce Pollution without Harmful Side Effects," found at www.ecopurer.com/pages/idea.html, accessed December 8, 2009.

10. Mathis Wackernagel and William Rees, *Our Ecological Footprint*, Gabriola Island, British Columbia, Canada: New Society Publishers, 1996.

11. William Rees, "Revisiting Carrying-Capacity: Area-Based Indicators of Sustainability," *Population and Environment* 17 (no. 3, January 1996):195–215.

12. For a review of metabolism studies of cities and the use of this framework in studying cities, see Christopher Kennedy, John Cuddihy, and Joshua Engel-Yan, "The Changing Metabolism of Cities," *Journal of Industrial Ecology* 11 (no. 2, 2007): 43–59. See also Abel Wolman, one of the first to write about the metabolism of cities: "The Metabolism of Cities," *Scientific American* 213 (no. 3, September 1965): 178–193.

13. "10 Buildings Inspired by the Natural World," posted by fixR, at www.fixr.com. 2009.

14. LAVA Architects, "Masdar Plaza, Oasis of the Future," project description, provided by the architects, p. 2.

15. Daily Mail, "The Floating Cities That Could One Day House Climate Change Refugees," *Daily Mail*, July 4, 2008.

16. "Santiago Calatrava, The Milwaukee Art Museum, Milwaukee, Wisconsin," found at www.arcspace.com/architects/calatrava/milwaukee_art_museum/, accessed December 7, 2009.

17. Quoted in Mike Chimo, "Spiraling Calatrava Chicago Tower to Be World's Second Tallest," found at www.inhabita.com, accessed June 11, 2009. The design incorporates the concepts of golden mean and the Fibonacci sequence.

18. Zaha Hadid, quoted in "Zaha Hadid Architects Unveil Design of New Abu Dhabi Performing Arts Centre," found at www.skyscrapercity.com/showthread.php?t=437630, accessed May 27, 2010.

19. Nicolai Ouroussoff, "Celebrating the Delicate Beauty of the Desert Landscape," *New York Times*, March 23, 2010, architectural review.

20. Penrith City, New South Wales, Australia, "Our Mascot—the Eastern Water Dragon," found at www.penrithcity.nsw.gov.au/index.asp?id=3048, accessed September 10, 2009.

21. Robert Putnam, *Bowling Alone: The Collapse and Revival of American Community*, New York: Simon and Shuster, 2001.

22. Kids in the Valley Adventuring!, found at kidsadventuring.org/blog/.

23. "Nature Strollers," found at www.naturestrollers.org/.

24. Urban Agriculture News, "44% of Vancouver Households Grow Food Says City Farmer," found at www.cityfarmer.org/44percent.html, accessed May 27, 2010.

25. Jan Gehl and Lars Gemzoe, *New City Spaces*, Copenhagen: Danish Architectural Press, 2008, p. 26.

26. Ibid., p. 40.

27. See Jan Gehl and Lars Gemzoe, *Public Spaces, Public Life,* Copenhagen: Danish Architectural Press, 1996.

28. City of Copenhagen, *Eco-Metropole: Our Vision for Copenhagen 2015,* Copenhagen, 2007.

29. See "About SPREE," found at www.spreeweb.org/home/about.html, accessed on March 13, 2010.

30. "VISTA: Strengthening Partnerships," *Learn and Serve Colorado,* December 2009, p. 4.

31. "Tokyo's 'Sea Forest' Project," *The Straits Times,* June 3, 2009.

32. City of Brisbane, Habitat Brisbane Program, 2007–2008 Annual Report, found at www.brisbane.qld.gov.au/bccwr/environment/documents/habitat_brisbane_annual_report_2008.pdf.

33. The objective of community cohesion is stated thus in the 2007–2008 annual report: "Increased sense of community fostered through the ownership, achievement and community pride created by participants joining together," Habitat Brisbane Program, p. 11. The results of a survey of participants support the achievement of this objective. Nearly 80% of respondents reported an increase in a sense of community (and 42% strongly agree that this is the case). See also Beatley, *Green Urbanism Down Under,* for a discussion of urban bushcare programs in a number of Australian cities.

34. *Tracks,* the newsletter of the Cleveland Museum of Natural History, vol. 37, no. 6, November/December 2009.

35. "Our Plastic Legacy Afloat," Editorial, *New York Times,* August 27, 2009.

36. See "Mayor Announces Plan to Reduce the Use of Tropical Hardwoods," February 11, 2008, found at www.NYC.gov, accessed February 17, 2009. See also Rohit Aggarwala, "Memorandum: Tropical Hardwood Reduction Plan," February 11, 2008.

37. Ibid.

38. There are sometimes legal obstacles to more sustainable and biophilic procurement. In the case of New York City, New York State General Municipal Law Sect. 103 actually forbids the city from making procurement decisions intended to advance a "social goal." As the city's Tropical Hardwood Reduction Plan states, "The use of certified sustainable wood is considered a 'social goal'. . . . Therefore it is illegal to specify FSC [Forest Stewardship Council] wood, or its equivalent, in bidding contracts" (p. 9). The only exception to this is for tropical hardwood species that are already banned by the state under its finance law.

39. See U.S. Fish and Wildlife Service, "Urban Conservation Treaty for Migratory Birds," Arlington, VA, April 2003; USFWS Press Release, "Urban Treaty for Bird Conservation Unveiled Tweety Named Official Spokesbird," June 13, 1999.

Chapter 4

1. David Owen, *Green Metropolis: Why Living Smaller, Living Closer, and Driving Less Are the Keys to Sustainability,* New York: Riverhead Books, 2009.

2. Ibid.

3. See Timothy Beatley, *Green Urbanism*, 2000, and *Native to Nowhere*, 2005.

4. www.bcn.es/turisme/english/turisme/rutes/colls_fr.htm.

5. For example, see City of Vancouver, *Vancouver Eco-Density Charter*, adopted by City Council, June 10, 2008.

6. Centre for Innovative Conservation Strategies, *Breaking the Barrier: Assessing the Value of Fauna-Friendly Crossing Structures at Compton Road,* a report to Brisbane City Council, November 2007.

7. See Tim Low, *Climate Change and Brisbane Biodiversity*, August 2007.

8. Nielsen and Hansen, "Do Green Areas Affect Health?" *Health and Place* 13 (2007):843.

9. USDA, 2004.

10. City of Brisbane, "Two Million Trees," found at www.brisbane.qld.gov.au/bccwr/environment/documents/regenerator_summer2008_2009.pdf.

11. American Forests, *Urban Ecosystem Analysis Atlanta Metro Area*, Washington, DC: American Forests, August 2001.

12. Blaine Harden, "Tree-Planting Drive Seeks to Bring a New Urban Cool," *Washington Post*, September 4, 2006, p. A01.

13. See American Forests at www.americanforests.org.

14. Maryland Department of Natural Resources, "A Report on Baltimore's Present and Potential Urban Tree Canopy," Annapolis: Maryland Forest Service, January 19, 2006.

15. See www.smud.org.

16. Pennsylvania Horticultural Society, "Tending the Urban Forest," summer 2006, found at www.pennsylvaniahorticulturalsociety.org/garden/ug_articleslist.html, accessed May 27, 2010.

17. For details about the program, see Pennsylvania Horticultural Society, "Tending the Urban Forest," summer 2006, found at www.pennsylvania horticulturalsociety.org/garden/ug_articleslist.html, accessed May 27, 2010.

18. For a review of some of these experiences, see Timothy Beatley, *Native to Nowhere*, Washington, DC: Island Press, 2005.

19. "Projects in Progress," found at www.plantsf.org/FeaturedProjects.html, accessed on November 2, 2009.

20. City of San Francisco, "Sidewalk Landscaping Permit, Information Sheet," Department of Public Works, Bureau of Urban Forestry, 2008.

21. See Friends of the High Line, www.thehighline.org/, accessed June 3, 2009.

22. From the online slide show, "High Line Design," found at www.thehighline.org/design/high-line-design, accessed June 3, 2009.

23. Salvador Rueda Palenzuela, *Barcelona, Ciudad Mediterranea, Compacta y Compleja: Una Vision de Future Mas Sostenible*, Barcelona: La Agencia de Ecologia Urbana, 2007.

24. Andrew Revkin, "Peeling Back Pavement to Expose Watery Havens," *New York Times*, July 16, 2009.

25. City of Los Angeles, *Los Angeles River Revitalization Master Plan*, City of Los Angeles, Department of Public Works, April 2007.

26. City of Richmond, Virginia, *Richmond Downtown Plan*, July 2009, p. 3.14.

27. Richard Pinkham, "Daylighting: New Life for Buried Streams," Snowmass, CO: Rocky Mountain Institute, 2000.

28. See Timothy Beatley, *Native to Nowhere*, Washington, DC: Island Press, 2005, for more detail on these projects.

29. City of Sydney, *Sustainable Sydney 2030*, Sydney, Australia, 2008.

30. UrbanLab, "Growing Water" presentation, found at www.urbanlab.com/h2o/, accessed May 21, 2009.

31. See City of Chicago, "Green Alleys," found at egov.cityofchicago.org/city/webportal/portalContentItemAction.do?topChannelName=HomePage&contentOID=536946345&Failed_Reason=Invalid+timestamp,+engine+has+been+restarted&contenTypeName=COC_EDITORIAL&com.broadvision.session.new=Yes&Failed_Page=/webp.

32. "A Hyper-Local Wine," *C'ville Weekly*, May 2009.

33. Cynthia Girling and Ronald Kellert, *Skinny Streets and Green Neighborhoods: Design for Environment and Community*, Washington, DC: Island Press, 2005.

34. See, for instance, Timothy Beatley, *Green Urbanism: Learning from European Cities*, Washington, DC: Island Press, 2000.

35. Chuck Davis and Tim Beatley, *The Nature of Cities*, documentary film, 2009.

36. For an extensive discussion of Vauban, see Timothy Beatley, *Native to Nowhere: Sustaining Home and Community in a Global Age*, Washington, DC: Island Press, 2005.

37. Isabelle Pommereau, *Christian Science Monitor*, December 21, 2006.

38. See Noisette Company, *Noisette Community Master Plan*, SC, pp. 2–3.

39. Noisette Foundation, *The Michaux Conservancy: A Noisette Foundation Strategic Initiative for Ecosystem Education and Restoration,* Charleston, SC, 2007, p. 4.

40. Kent State University's Cleveland Urban Design Collaborative, *Re-Imagining a More Sustainable Cleveland*, Cleveland, OH: adopted by the Cleveland Planning Commission, December 19, 2008.

41. Ibid., p. 3.

42. Kent State University's Cleveland Urban Design Collaborative, *Re-Imagining Cleveland Vacant Land Re-Use Pattern Book*, Cleveland, OH: April 2009.

43. The classic study is Roger Ulrich, "View through a Window May Influence Recovery from Surgery, *Science*, 224, April 27, 1984.

44. See Judith Heerwegen, "Do Green Buildings Enhance the Well Being of Workers?" *Environmental Design and Construction Magazine*, January 2001, found at www.edcmag.com/CDA/Archives/fb077b7338697010VgnVCM100000f932a 8c0____, accessed March 12, 2010.

45. See www.melbourne.vic.gov.au/Environment/CH2/Evaluation/Pages/Evaluation.aspx; also see Timothy Beatley, *Green Urbanism Down Under: Learning from Australia's Sustainable Communities*, Washington, DC: Island Press, 2008.

46. Bank of America, "Bank of America Tower Project Fact Sheet," 2007, found at newsroom.bankofamerica.com/...bankofamerica/.../OBP+Project+Fact+Sheet_040507.pdf, accessed October 14, 2009.

47. For more detail about this building, see Bettina von Hagen, Erin Kellogg, and Eugenie Frerichs, eds., *Rebuilt Green: The Natural Capital Center and the Transformative Power of Building*, Portland, OR: Ecotrust, 2003.

48. Mike Archer and Bob Beale, *Going Native*, Sydney: University of New South Wales Press, 2004, pp. 334–335.

49. For a very good review of the benefits of green rooftops and a review of research about their environmental effectiveness, see Kristin L. Getter and D. Bradley Rowe, "The Role of Extensive Roofs in Sustainable Development," *HortScience* 41 (no. 5, 2006):1276–1285.

50. See Green Roofs for Healthy Cities, at www.greenroofs.org/index.php/annualconferences, accessed December 22, 2009.

51. Stephan Brenneisen, "Space for Urban Wildlife: Designing Green Roofs as Habitats in Switzerland," *Urban Habitats* 4 (no. 1, 2006):31.

52. Cliff Kuang, "8-Story Antigravity Forest Façade Takes Root, *Wired Magazine*, August 24, 2009.

53. Kristen Hohenadel, "All His Rooms Are Living Rooms," *New York Times*, May 3, 2007, Section F, p. 1.

54. Research indicates that this wall is likely to remove half of the benzene in the air and some 90% of the formaldehyde; see University of Guelph.

55. The next several paragraphs are drawn from Timothy Beatley, "Toward Biophilic Cities," in Kellert, Heerwegen, and Mador, eds., *Biophilic Design*, Hoboken, NJ: John Wiley and Sons, 2008.

56. Kieran Timberlake, "Middle School, Addition and Renovation, Sidwell Friends, Washington, District of Columbia," found at www.Kierantimberlake.com/pl_education/sidwell_school_1.html, accessed December 16, 2009. The building uses some 90% less water than a typical school of similar size and 60% less energy. See also Rebecca Barnes, "Earth-Friendly School," *The Christian Science Monitor*, March 11, 2008.

57. Ibid.

58. Jane Brody, "Turning the Ride to School Into a Walk," *New York Times*, September 11, 2007.

59. Auckland Regional Transport Authority, "Walking School Bus," found at citiesofmigration.ca/the wonders-of-walking-walking school0bus-programme/lang/en, accessed September 7, 2009.

60. See Auckland Regional Transit Authority, "Auckland's Waking School Buses Meet Oceania Stars," found at www.travelwise.org.nz/NewsAndEvents/index, December 5, 2008; see also Damian Collins and Robin A. Kearns, "Walking School Buses in the Auckland Region: A Longitudinal Assessment," *Transport Policy*, 2009.

Chapter 5

1. Chicago Landscape Ordinance, found at egov.cityofchicago.org/city/webportal/portalContentItemAction.do?blockName=Promo+Item&

channelId=536899053&programId=536888905&topChannelName=Business&
contentOID=536910033&Failed_Reason=Invalid+timestamp,+engine+has+
been+restarted&contenTypeName=COC_EDITORIAL&com.broadvision
.session.new=Yes&Failed_Page=%2fwebportal%2fportalContentItemAction.do, accessed March 13, 2010.

2. David A. Taylor, "Growing Green Roofs, City by City," *Environmental Health
Perspectives* 115 (no. 6, June 2007):A308–A311.

3. By-law No. 583-2009; see City of Toronto, "Green Roof Bylaw," found at
www.toronto.ca/greenroofs/overview.html, accessed November 20, 2009.

4. See City of Berlin, "Biotope Area Factor," found at www.stadtentwicklung
.berlin.de/umwelt/landschaftsplanung/bff/en/berechnungsbeispiele.shtml.

5. See City of Seattle, "Seattle Green Factor," found at www.seattle.gov/dpd/
permits/greenfactor/Overview/.

6. City of Seattle, "Director's Report and Recommendations: Commercial
Code Clean-up Amendments," March 9, 2009.

7. As an example, K. L. Getter and D. B. Rowe report that the German city of
Esslingen will cover up to half the cost of installing a new green roof there. See
Getter and Rowe, "Effect of Substrate Depth and Planting Season on Sedum Plug
Establishment for Extensive Green Roofs," Proceedings of the Fifth North Ameri-
can Green Roof Conference: Greening Rooftops for Sustainable Communities,
Minneapolis, 2007.

8. See Portland Metropolitan Services District, "Nature in Neighborhoods
Capital Grants," found at www.oregonmetro.gov/index.cfm/go/by.web/id=
18203.

9. See Portland Metropolitan Services District, "Nature in Neighborhoods,"
found at www.oregonmetro.gov/index.cfm/go/by.web/id+13745, accessed September 7, 2009.

10. Portland Metro, "Nature in Neighborhood Restoration and Enhancement Grants," found at www.oregonmetro.gov/index.cfm/go/by.web/id=24982,
accessed on May 28, 2010.

11. See City of Greensboro, NC, "Greensboro Water Resources," found at
www.greensboro-nc.gov/departments/Water/customer/stormwaterrates.htm, accessed March 2, 2010.

12. Community Boating Inc., "Mission," found at www.communityboating
.org/mission.php, accessed October 7, 2009.

13. Barbara Shema, "Learn to Sail at Community Boating Programs," Suite
101.com.

14. For instance, in California, under the Mello-Roos Community Facilities Act
of 1982, localities can create public facility districts, float bonds to pay for a variety
of community improvements, and property owners agree to tax themselves over
20 years to pay debt service on the bonds. Berkeley was the first jurisdiction in
California to use this authority specifically to provide upfront financing for solar
energy systems, under its Berkeley FIRST program.

15. Ashoka Community Greens, *Alley Gating and Greening Toolkit Baltimore*,
written by Benjamin Nathanson and Danielle Emmet, edited by Kate Harrod, found

at www.cleanergreenerbaltimore.org/.../Toolkit%20%20Latham%20OK%20Ver% 205%200x.pdf.

16. "Measuring Impact," at www.communitygreens.org/measuringimpact, accessed October 15, 2009. "After alley gating and greening, properties abutting alley greens tend to increase in value by 5% to 15%. As a result, these blocks with alley greens attract new homeowners and therefore decrease the number of vacant and abandoned houses in the area. In addition, higher home values increase real estate revenues benefiting the entire community," p. 7, *Alley Gating and Greening Toolkit*.

17. Jan C. Semenza, "The Intersection of Urban Planning, Art, and Public Health: The Sunnyside Piazza," *American Journal of Public Health* 93 (no. 9, September 2003):1439–1441.

18. "Pavement to Parks," found at sfpavementtoparks.sfplanning.org/, accessed December 16, 2009.

19. Ibid.

20. Michael M. Grynbaum, "A Closing on Broadway Becomes Permanent," *New York Times*, February 10, 2010.

21. Under Sadik-Khan's leadership, bike lane miles have almost doubled in about two years; see Kuitenbrouwer, "NYC Transit Chief Eager to See Streetcars; She's Making Her City a Better Place to Talk, Cycle," *National Post*, Toronto Edition, April 22, 2009.

22. Joe Nasr, presentation, University of Virginia, November 30, 2009.

23. For a review of state "Leave No Child Inside" laws and initiatives, see Allen Cooper, "Children and the Outdoors: State Policy Solutions Guide," National Wildlife Federation, 2008.

24. This is an abbreviated list; for the complete text of the Chicago Wilderness "Children's Outdoor Bill of Rights," see www.kidsoutside.info/billofrights/, accessed June 2, 2009.

25. Ibid.

26. Examples of such maps include a map of the Cuyahoga Bioregion, prepared by EcoCity Cleveland, and at smaller neighborhood scale, a map of the Pimmit Run watershed, in Arlington County, Virginia. See Timothy Beatley, *Native to Nowhere*, for discussion of both.

27. NYC Green Codes Task Force, Executive Summary, found at www .urbangreencouncil.org/greencodes/, accessed March 13, 2010.

28. The report specifically recommends a requirement that at least half of the nonbuilt area of a new development be designed to be permeable.

29. Amina Khan, "Orange Officials Sue Couple Who Removed Their Lawn," *Los Angeles Times*, March 2, 2010.

30. Ann Cameron Siegal, "Bats Be Gone!" *Washington Post*, September 19, 2009, p. E1.

31. The month following the Los Angeles attack, a Canadian singer, Taylor Mitchell, was apparently attacked and killed by coyotes while hiking in Nova Scotia. This will undoubtedly give support to those who advise a more cautious route

and extermination when in doubt. But the circumstances of the Mitchell attack are unclear and may have involved one or more rabid coyotes, or at least coyotes who were young and desperately hungry. And there is some speculation that the animals might have been wolf–coyote hybrids and that the victim may have assumed a prey posture by running. Still, this was only the second human death from coyotes ever reported in North America, speaking again to the highly improbable danger associated with what are usually very shy animals.

32. See Junior Natural Program, the Wildlife Center, www.wildwnc.org/information/junior-naturalist.

33. Cleveland Botanical Garden, "Green Corps Urban Learning Farms." Undated, p. 1.

34. Ibid.

35. Brooklyn Botanic Garden, "Greenest Block in Brooklyn," found at www.bbg.org/edu/greenbridge/greenestblock/, accessed August 31, 2009.

36. Brooklyn Botanic Garden, "Deadline for Entering the Annual Greenest Block in Brooklyn Contest is Monday, June 1," www.bbg.org, May 15, 2009.

37. See Pennsylvania Horticultural Society, "Tending the Urban Forest," Philadelphia, 2007.

38. "Residents will use the skills they acquire to become stewards of their neighborhoods. The project is off to a vibrant start with engaged citizens, eager partners, and a solid vision for a greener, more sustainable future." *Annual Report*, Pennsylvania Horticultural Society, 2009, p. 17. Funding for this initiative is coming from Home Depot Foundation, the Local Initiatives Support Corporation, the William Penn Foundation, and the Philadelphia Water Department.

39. For example, see "Ten Years Later: NYRP's Community Garden Program Is Growing Stronger," *Gooddirt, the NYRP Newsletter,* Spring/Summer, 2009, p. 1.

40. Personal communication with Sara Borgstrom, October 14, 2008.

41. For example, see Richmond Audubon Society, www.richmondaudubon.org/index.html.

42. Citizens are encouraged to pledge to take one of seven actions: plant drought-resistant plants, plant a mixed hedgerow, plant a broad-leaved tree, make a pond, use mulch, add a green roof to your shed, and wild up your decking; see London Wildlife Trust, www.wildlondon.org.uk/gardening/Home/tabid/384/Default.aspx, accessed June 1, 2010.

43. For a full history of the organization, see Washington Biologists' Field Club, *The Washington Biologists' Field Club: Its Members and Its History (1900–2006)*, Mathew C. Perry ed., 2007.

Chapter 6

1. Kristina Hill, "Designing the Urban Ark," lecture to the Harvard Museum of Natural History, March 2009.

2. "Birds and Climate Change: On the Move," *The Thrasher*, March/April 29, Richmond Audubon Society, found at http://www.richmondaudubon.org/ThrasherBackIssues.html, accessed May 28, 2010.

3. One thinks of research similar to Richard Levine's work gauging the pace of life in different cities and the creative experiments he designed to gauge this. See Richard V. Levine, *A Geography of Time*, New York: Basic Books, 2006.

4. Singapore has taken the lead in developing the rating system, and there is a draft set of indicators and a user's manual, see *Draft User's Manual for the Singapore Index on Cities' Biodiversity*, June 2009, found at www.cbd.int/.../cities/cities-draft-user-manual-singapore-index-2009-07-01-en.pdf.

5. Eric Sanderson, *Mannahatta: A Natural History of New York City*, New York: Abrams, 2009.

6. Mike Leggett, "Quickly Identify Plants, Birds with iPhone Apps," February 3, found at www.statesman.com/sports/outdoors/quickly-identify-plants-birds-with-iphone-apps-212065.html, accessed February 26, 2010.

7. Ryan Kim, "Augmenting How We See the World," *San Francisco Chronicle*, October 26, 2009, front page, p. A1.

8. Ibid., p. A8.

9. Stephen Kellert interview, in *The Nature of Cities*, documentary film, 2009.

Bibliography

American Forests. 2001. *Urban Ecosystem Analysis Atlanta Metro Area*, Washington, DC: American Forests, August.

American Planning Association. 2006. *Planning and Urban Design Standards*, Hoboken, NJ: John Wiley and Sons.

Archer, Mike and Bob Beale. 2004. *Going Native*, Sydney: Hodder.

Barnes, Rebecca. 2008. "Earth-Friendly School," *The Christian Science Monitor*, March 11.

Beatley, Timothy. 2000. *Green Urbanism: Learning from European Cities*, Washington, DC: Island Press.

Beatley, Timothy. 2004. *Native to Nowhere*, Washington, DC: Island Press.

Beatley, Timothy, with Peter Newman. 2008. *Green Urbanism Down Under: Learning from Australia's Sustainable Communities,* Washington, DC: Island Press.

Benyus, Janine. 2002. *Biomimicry: Innovation Inspired by Nature*, New York: Harper Perennial.

Berry, Thomas. 2006. *Evening Thoughts: Reflecting on Earth as Sacred Community*, San Francisco: Sierra Club Books.

Blanc, Patrick. 2008. *The Vertical Garden: From Nature to the City*, New York: Norton and Company.

Brenneisen, Stephan. 2006. "Space for Urban Wildlife: Designing Green Roofs as Habitats in Switzerland," *Urban Habitats* 4(1).

Brodo, Irwin M., Sylvia Duran Sharnoff, and Stephen Sharnoff. 2001. *Lichens of North America*, New Haven, CT: Yale University Press.

Bryant, Salatheia. 2006. "Bats Make Some Uneasy in Wake of Rabies Case; Despite News of Boy's Infection, Creatures Mostly Avoid People, Experts Say." *The Houston Chronicle*, May 11, p. A16.

Campbell, Marcia Caton and Danielle A. Salus. 2003. "Community and Conservation Land Trusts as Unlikely Partners? The Case of Troy Gardens, Madison, Wisconsin," *Land Use Policy* 20:169–180.

Carson, Rachel. 1956. "Help Your Child to Wonder," *Woman's Home Companion*, July.

Chivian, Eric and Aaron Bernstein, eds. 2008. *Sustaining Life: How Human Health Depends on Biodiversity*, Oxford: Oxford University Press.

City of Copenhagen. 2007. *Eco-Metropole: Our Vision for Copenhagen 2015.*

City of Los Angeles. 2007. *Los Angeles River Revitalization Master Plan*, draft, January, Los Angeles Public Works Department.

City of New York. 2008. *PlaNYC: A Greener, Greater New York*, New York City Mayor's Office.

City of Oakland. 2006. "A Food Systems Assessment for Oakland, CA: Toward a Sustainable Food Plan," May 24, prepared by Serena Unger and Heather Wooten.

City of Richmond, Virginia. 2009. *Richmond Downtown Plan*, July.

City of Sydney, Australia. 2008. *Sustainable Sydney 2030.*

City of Toronto. Undated. "Bird Friendly Development Rating System and Acknowledgement Program," found at https://wx.toronto.ca/inter/plan/birdfriendly.nsf/Rating?OpenForm.

Cleveland Museum of Natural History. 2008. *Reinventing the Natural History Museum for the Future, Annual Report, 2007–2008*, Cleveland, June 17.

Costanza, Robert, Octavio Pérez-Maqueo, M. Luisa Martinez, Paul Sutton, Sharolyn J. Anderson, and Kenneth Mulder. 2008. "The Value of Coastal Wetlands for Hurricane Protection," *AMBIO: A Journal of the Human Environment* 37(4):241–248.

Crowe, John H., Folkert A. Hoekstra, and Lois M. Crowe. 1992. "Anhydrobiosis," *Annual Review of Physiology* 54:579–599.

Day, Leslie. 2007. *Field Guide to the Natural World of New York City*, Baltimore, MD: Johns Hopkins University Press.

Dean, Tom. 2004. "Finding Devonian," in *Living with Topsoil: Tending Spirits, Cherishing Land*, North Liberty, IA: Ice Cube Press.

Delgadillo, Claudio and Angeles Cardenas. 2000. "Urban Mosses in Mexico City," *Anales del Instituto de Biologia Universidad Nacional Autonoma de Mexico*, Serie Botanica 71(2):63–72.

Dobson, Frank. 2006. *Guide to Common Urban Lichens*, Part 1: *On Trees and Wood*, and Part 2: *On Stones and Soil*, Field Studies Council.

Dreiseitl, Herbert. and Dieter Grau, eds. 2005. *New Waterscapes: Planning, Building and Designing with Water*, Birkhäuser Basel.

FORMAS. 2005. *Sustainable City of Tomorrow*, Stockholm, Sweden: Formas.

Gehl, Jan and Lars Gemzoe. 2008. *New City Spaces*, Copenhagen: Danish Architectural Press.

Getter, Kristin L. and D. Bradley Rowe. 2006. "The Role of Extensive Roofs in Sustainable Development," *HortScience* 41(5):1276–1285.

Girling, Cynthia and Ronald Kellett. 2005. *Skinny Streets and Green Neighborhoods: Design for Environment and Community*, Washington, DC: Island Press.

Greater London Authority. 2007. *The Mayor's Climate Change Action Plan*, London, February.

Gruchow, Paul. 1995. *Grass Roots: The Universe of Home*, Minneapolis, MN: Milkweed Editions.

Haq, Amber. 2006. "Redefining the Urban Jungle," *Business Week Online*, October 5.

Harden, Blaine. 2006. "Tree-planting Drive Seeks to Bring a New Urban Cool," *The Washington Post*, September 4, p. A01.

Hartig, Terry and H. Staats. 2006. "The Need for Psychological Restoration as a Determinant of Environmental Preferences," *Journal of Environmental Psychology* 26:215–226.

Helm, Morgan E. 2009. "Denver's Street Smart Prairie Dogs," www .smithsonianmag.com/science-nature/Denvers-Street-Smart-Prairie-Dogs .html, accessed October 2.

Hough, Michael. 1995. *Cities and Natural Process*, New York: Routledge Press.

Karbabi, Barbara. 2005. "Bats over Bayou: The Park People Take Sightseers to the Waugh Drive Bridge, Where the Furry Creatures Hang Out until Dusk; The Stars Come Out at Night and Take Flight," *The Houston Chronicle*, Nov. 15, Star, p. 4.

Kaufman, Jerome and Martin Bailkey. 2004. "Farming Inside Cities through Entrepreneurial Urban Agriculture," in Rosalind Greenstein and Yesim Sungu-Eryilmaz, *Recycling the City: The Use and Reuse of Urban Land*, Cambridge, MA: Lincoln Institute of Land Policy.

Kellert, Stephen. 2006. *Building for Life: Designing and Understanding the Human–Nature Connection*, Washington, DC: Island Press.

Kellert, Stephen, Judith Heerwagen, and Marty Mador, eds. 2008. *Biophilic Design: The Theory, Science and Practice of Bringing Buildings to Life*, New York: John Wiley.

Kellert, Stephen and E. O. Wilson. 1993. *The Biophilia Hypothesis*, Washington, DC: Island Press.

Kennedy, Christopher, John Cuddihy, and Joshua Engel-Yan. 2007. "The Changing Metabolism of Cities," *Journal of Industrial Ecology* 11(2):43–59.

Kent State University's Cleveland Urban Design Collaborative. 2008. *Re-Imagining A More Sustainable Cleveland*, Cleveland, Ohio, adopted by the Cleveland Planning Commission, December 19, 2008.

Kent State University's Cleveland Urban Design Collaborative. 2009. *Re-Imagining Cleveland Vacant Land Re-Use Pattern Book*, Cleveland, Ohio, April.

Kinchin, Ian M. 1994. *The Biology of Tardigrades*, Surrey, UK: Ashgate Publishers.

King County, Washington. 2008. *King County Biodiversity Report*, Seattle: King County.

Leather, Phil, Mike Pyrgas, Di Beale, and Claire Lawrence. 1998. "Windows in the Workplace: Sunlight, View, and Occupational Stress," *Environment and Behavior* 30(6, November):739–762.

Louv, Richard. 2005. *Last Child in the Woods*. Chapel Hill, NC: Algonquin Books.

Low, Nicholas, Brenan Gleeson, Ray Green, and Darko Rodovic. 2005. *The Green City: Sustainable Homes, Sustainable Suburbs*, Sydney: UNSW Press.

Marler, Peter R. and Hans Slabbekoorn. 2004. *Nature's Music: The Science of Birdsong*, San Diego: Elsevier Academic Press.

Maryland Department of Natural Resources. 2006. "A Report on Baltimore's City's Present and Potential Urban Tree Canopy," Annapolis: Maryland Forest Service, January 19.

McDonough, William and Michael Braungart. 2002. *Cradle to Cradle: Remaking the Way We Make Things*, New York: North Point Press.

Nelson, Arthur C. 2006. "Leadership in a New Era," *Journal of the American Planning Association* 72(4, Autumn):393–407.

Nielsen, Thomas Sick and Kartsen Bruun Hansen. 2007. "Do Green Areas Affect Health?" *Health and Place* 13:843.

Newman, Peter and Jeffrey Kenworthy. 1999. *Sustainability and Cities*, Washington, DC: Island Press.

Pagano, Michael A. and Ann O'M. Bowman. 2000. *Vacant Land in Cities: An Urban Resource,* Washington, DC: Brookings Institution Center on Metropolitan Policy.

Palenzuela, Salvador Rueda. 2007. *Barcelona, Ciudad Mediterranea, Compacta y Compleja: Una Vision de Future Mas Sostenible*, Barcelona: La Agencia de Ecologia Urbana.

Parker, John. 2009. "An Analysis of Urban Ecological Knowledge and Behavior in Wellington, New Zealand," MA thesis, Victoria University, Wellington, New Zealand, found at researcharchive.vuw.ac.nz/bitstream/handle/10063/1263/thesis.pdf?...1.

Parks and People Foundation. Undated. *Creating an Urban Ecosystem of Green and Blue Spaces in Baltimore,* Baltimore: Parks and People Foundation.

Pinkham, Richard. 2000. "Daylighting: New Life for Buried Streams," Snowmass, CO: Rocky Mountain Institute.

Preston, Richard. 2007. *The Wild Trees: A Story of Passion and Daring*, New York: Random House.

Pyle, Robert M. 1993. *The Thunder Tree: Lessons from an Urban Wildland*. New York: Lyons Press.

Revkin, Andrew. 2009. "Peeling Back Pavement to Expose Watery Havens," *New York Times,* July 17.

Rizzo, Larry. 2001. *Kansas City Wildlands,* Jefferson City: Conservation Commission of the State of Missouri.

Ryerson University. 2005. *Report on the Environmental Benefits and Costs of Green Roof Technology for the City of Toronto*, prepared for the City of Toronto, Department of Architecture, Ryerson University, Toronto, October 31.

Sanderson, Eric. 2009. *Mannahatta: A Natural History of New York City,* New York: Abrams.

Schantz, Peter and Erik Stigell. 2008. "Are Green Elements Principal Pull Factors for Physical Activity?" The Research Unit for Movement, Health and Environment, The Swedish School for Sport and Health Sciences, Stockholm, summary of a presentation, supplied by the author.

Schinkel, Walter R. 2004. "The Nest Architecture of the Florida Harvester Ant, *Pogonomyrmes," Journal of Insect Science* 4:21.

Schwartz, Anne. "Good Parks Are Good for the Economy," *Gotham Gazette,* June 2009.

Setterblad, Martin and Annika Kruuse. 2006. "Design and Biodiversity. A Brown Field Roof in Malmö, Sweden," Malmö, Sweden, unpublished paper.

Seymour, Mona and Jennifer Wolch. 2009. "Toward Zoöpolis? Innovation and Contradiction in a Conservation Community," *Journal of Urbanism* 2 (no. 3, November):215–236.

Sipman, H. J. M. 2009. "Tropical Urban Lichens: Observations from Singapore," *Blumea—Biodiversity, Evolution and Biogeography of Plants* 54 (nos. 1–3, October):297–299.

Stilgoe, John R. 1998. *Outside Lies Magic: Regaining History and Awareness in Everyday Places*, New York: Walker and Company.

Tallmadge, John. 2004. *The Cincinnati Arch: Learning from Nature in the City*, Athens: University of Georgia Press.

Taylor, Andrea Faber, et al. 1998. "Growing Up in the Inner City: Green Spaces as Places to Grow," *Environment and Behavior* 30(1, January):3–27.

Taylor, David A. 2007. "Growing Green Roofs, City by City," *Environmental Health Perspectives* 115(6, June):A308–A311.

University of Guelph. 2004. "Guelph–Humber Plant Wall a Breath of Fresh Air," *At Guelph* 48(17).

USDA Forest Service. 2004. "The Value of Trees," Statistics Sheet, Urban and Community Forestry Appreciation Tool Kit.

Wilson, E. O. 1984. *Biophilia*, Cambridge, MA: Harvard University Press.

Wilson, E. O. 1993. "Biophilia and the Conservation Ethic," in Stephen Kellert and E. O. Wilson, *Biophilia: The Human Bond with Other Species*, Cambridge, MA: Harvard University Press.

Wilson, E. O. 2006. *The Creation: An Appeal to Save Life on Earth*, New York: Norton.

Wolch, Jennifer. 1996. "Zoöpolis," *Capitalism Nature Socialism* 7 (2, June):21–47.

Index

Figures/photos/illustrations are indicated by a " f."